Culture, politics and local government in Fingal, 1891–1914

Maynooth Studies in Local History

SERIES EDITOR Raymond Gillespie

This volume is one of six short books published in the Maynooth Studies in Local History series in 2017. Like their predecessors they range widely, both chronologically and geographically, over the local experience in the Irish past. Chronologically they span the worlds of early modern Kerry, 18th-century Stradbally, in Laois, and those of Dublin and Cork in the early 20th century. Geographically they range across the length of the country from Dublin to Cork and westwards to the Atlantic world of Kerry. Socially they move from the landed and elite society of Castle Hyde and Stradbally Hall to the social position of the 20th-century Cork women street traders and Dublin tenement dwellers and examining the experience of the rising middle class in Fingal. In doing so they reveal diverse and complicated societies that created the local past and present the range of possibilities open to anyone interested in studying that past. Those possibilities involve the dissection of the local experience in the complex and contested social worlds of which it is part as people strove to preserve and enhance their positions within their local societies. Such studies of local worlds over such long periods are vital for the future since they not only stretch the historical imagination but provide a longer perspective on the evolution of society in Ireland and help us to understand more fully the complex evolution of the Irish experience. These works do not simply chronicle events relating to an area within administrative or geographically determined boundaries, but open the possibility of understanding how and why particular regions had their own personality in the past. Such an exercise is clearly one of the most exciting challenges for the future and demonstrates the vitality of the study of local history in Ireland.

Like their predecessors, these six short books are reconstructions of the socially diverse worlds of the poor as well as the rich, women as well as men, the geographical marginal as well as those located near the centre of power. They examine the way in which those who inhabited those worlds lived their daily lives, often little affected by the large themes that dominate the writing of national history. In addressing these issues, studies such as those presented in these short books, together with their predecessors, are at the forefront of Irish historical research and represent some of the most innovative and exciting work being undertaken in Irish history today. They also provide models which others can follow up and adapt in their own studies of the Irish past. In such ways will we understand better the regional diversity of Ireland and the social and cultural basis for that diversity. These books, with their predecessors, convey the vibrancy and excitement of the world of Irish local history today.

Maynooth Studies in Local History: Number 128

Culture, politics and local government in Fingal, 1891–1914

Declan Brady

FOUR COURTS PRESS

Set in 10pt on 12pt Bembo by
Carrigboy Typesetting Services for
FOUR COURTS PRESS LTD
7 Malpas Street, Dublin 8, Ireland
www.fourcourtspress.ie
and in North America for
FOUR COURTS PRESS
c/o ISBS, 920 N.E. 58th Avenue, Suite 300, Portland, OR 97213

ISBN 978-1-84682-641-2

Printed in Ireland
by SprintPrint, Dublin.

Contents

Acknowledgments

I would like to thank the following people, without whom this project could not have been undertaken. I would like to express thanks to my MA supervisor, Professor Terence Dooley, for his advice and encouragement but also his direction, confidence in my ability, and enthusiasm for the subject, which is truly infectious. A note of appreciation is also due to Professor Marian Lyons for the exhortation to take on such challenging material. It has been a rewarding journey. Finally, thank you to Professor Raymond Gillespie for the invitation to be part of the company of scholarly endeavour that is the Maynooth Studies in Local History series.

The staff of the National Library of Ireland, National Archives of Ireland, Maynooth University Library, UCD Archives & Library, Dublin City Archives and Fingal County Libraries have been at all times helpful and courteous. I am grateful to Dr Colm Quinn and Jacinta Judge of Fingal Local Studies and County Archives for their assistance, availability and knowledge, and the permission to reproduce documents in this book.

I am most grateful for the experience of engaging with the teaching staff of the department of history at Maynooth University and my fellow students, which opened up many valuable insights and perspectives, which I have been able to draw upon for this work.

I would like to thank Phil McCabe of Killester College of Further Education for her initial encouragement to pursue further research and study, and Bernadette Marks of Swords Historical Society for her insights and for sharing her knowledge of Fingal local history.

As a mark of my appreciation, this book is dedicated to my wife Ann and my children, Liam, Eoghan and Rory, without whose support, encouragement and patience this work could not have been attempted.

Introduction

This short volume in the Maynooth Studies in Local History Series is based on a 2015 Master's thesis that drew its inspiration from primary research that I undertook for a series of local history walking tours on early 20th-century life in the town of Swords, Co. Dublin. Local history can provide invaluable perspective in understanding important historical periods, particularly those intervening periods of decline, consolidation or growth between momentous events. The period between the fall of Parnell and the outbreak of the First World War saw the fracturing of the Irish Parliamentary Party, and the void of political focus it caused, filled by a more radical discourse influenced by the cultural and literary revivals and the development of an informed nationalist identity and purpose. Progressive legislation in the areas of land purchase, local government, and education facilitated the movement into local politics of an advanced nationalist cohort, from within and without constitutional nationalism, and prompted the withdrawal of the traditional landed elite from positions of local influence. Examining these elites, their composition, connections, politics and socio-cultural networks in north Dublin, as Ireland and its identity were changing, can illuminate the nature, causes and extent of that change. The period is free of major violent episodes, with changing local influence steadily traceable over time as land ownership shifted and local electoral politics became increasingly representative and accountable.

Placing systematic and extensive local primary research in the context of national secondary historiography, this study examines the shift in elite influence through the leading personalities involved in Fingal local politics from 1891 to 1914. The original records of successive local government bodies, the Co. Dublin grand jury, Balrothery poor law union, Balrothery and north Dublin rural district councils and Dublin county council are available in the manuscript room at Fingal County Archives and in the National Archives of Ireland. Archival evidence from political and cultural groups such as the United Irish League, Sinn Féin, the Unionist Convention, North County Dublin Farmers Association, the Gaelic Athletic Association and the Gaelic League is supplemented by detailed newspaper coverage and police intelligence reports. Consulting so wide a range of primary sources balances some of the inevitable bias of the different authors. Extensive consultation of British House of Commons parliamentary papers in relation to the fixing of judicial rents and advances made under the various land purchase acts presents specific evidence of the shift in prosperity. Detailed analysis of 25 years of the *Drogheda Independent* presents Fingal life in the context of its time, just as national titles offer the corresponding national and Dublin city perspectives. Use of Bureau of Military History witness statements and military service pension records relating to the officers of the Fingal Brigade who mustered in 1916 aids discovery of the paths taken by those individuals in the years leading to the rebellion. Analysis of the 1901 and 1911 census returns, and genealogical records, helps to locate individuals and trace relationships.

The historiography of Fingal in the period is poor, with no significant academic survey and only a small number of local or event-specific histories. The general literature substantially covers the two political creeds that dominated in Ireland in the period, unionism and nationalism, the extremes of which, Ulster unionism and Irish republicanism, and their respective interactions with British rule, determined Ireland's destiny. *A new history of Ireland: Ireland under the union, 1870–1921* (Oxford, 1996), edited by W.E. Vaughan, provides the authoritative narrative of the period. The chapters by F.S.L. Lyons are of particular relevance.[1] Lyons also explores the national dimension in *Ireland since the Famine* (London, 1971). More recent contributions are Alvin Jackson, *Ireland, 1798–1998: politics and war* (Oxford, 1999) and Paul Bew, *The politics of enmity, 1789–2000* (Oxford, 2007). Thematic and interpretive insights by experienced historians such as Joseph Lee, D. George Boyce, R.V. Comerford, David Fitzpatrick and Pauric Travers offer different perspectives on similar themes, as material is re-examined and revisited.[2] Paul Bew highlights the struggle within constitutional nationalism itself, between conciliatory and militant factions, the Irish Parliamentary Party being a coalition of Dillonite agrarians, Devlinite Catholic nationalists and Redmondite home rulers,[3] in *Conflict and conciliation in Ireland, 1890–1910: Parnellites and radical agrarians* (Oxford, 1987). The land question remains prominent, and the situation in Fingal was somewhat different to that in the rest of the country, as we shall observe; given its proximity to Dublin city and strong tillage bias, it exhibited labour as well as tenant tensions. Literature on the land issue, such as W.E. Vaughan, *Landlords and tenants in Ireland, 1848–1904* (Dundalk, 1984) and Philip Bull, *Land, politics and nationalism: a study of the Irish land question* (Dublin, 1996), focuses on the national perspective, but provides the backdrop against which the Fingal experience can be measured. *Ireland: land, politics and people* (Cambridge, 1982), edited by P.J. Drudy, and *Irish peasants: violence and political unrest, 1780–1914* (Madison, WI, 2003), edited by Samuel Clark and James S. Donnelly Jnr, contain more material pertinent to understanding events in Fingal. *A labour history of Ireland, 1824–2000* (Dublin, 2011), by Emmet O'Connor, details the evolution of the labour movement – the two chapters covering 1889–1916 are of particular relevance – while Padraig Yeates' *Lockout: Dublin 1913* (Dublin, 2001) is the definitive account of the Lockout. A number of important essays by Padraig Lane give explicit insight into the labourers' plight.[4]

The decline of the big house in Ireland: a study of Irish landed families, 1860–1960 (Dublin, 2001) by Terence Dooley relates the landlords' perspective and was particularly useful in this study in defining and characterizing the landed elite and local hierarchies.[5] There is a growing body of academic work on Catholic elites and the evolution of the revolutionary movement. Senia Pašeta's *Before the revolution: nationalism, social change and Ireland's Catholic elite, 1879–1922* (Cork, 1999) identified the Catholic intelligentsia that saw themselves as the government-in-waiting after home rule, only to be deprived of the prize after 1916 by an alternative republican nationalist rival. Fergus Campbell, in *The Irish establishment, 1879–1914* (Oxford, 2009), exhaustively reviews Catholic upward professional mobility and concludes that there was a closed elite, blocking Catholic accession to the highest levels of the establishment, a finding that contradicts earlier contentions by McDowell and McBride.[6] Ciaran O'Neill, in *Catholics of consequence: transnational education, social mobility and the Irish Catholic elite, 1850–1900* (Oxford, 2014), shows the lengths to which some went to break in to that establishment. Patrick Maume's *The long gestation: Irish nationalist life, 1891–1918* (Dublin, 1999) relates the continuing evolution of Irish politics after Parnell and the importance of newspapers in spreading the nationalist message. He tells how the controlling nature and closed elitism of the Irish Parliamentary Party led to disaffection and generated opposition and antagonism to British governance in Ireland. Fearghal McGarry and Roy Foster, respectively, evoke the intellectual dynamism of Dublin in the decade prior to the 1916 Rising, in the early parts of their recent narratives, *The Rising: Ireland: Easter 1916* (Oxford, 2011) and *Vivid faces: the revolutionary generation in Ireland, 1890–1923* (London, 2014). Detailed studies of the revolutionary movement such as Leon Ó Broin's *Revolutionary underground: the story of the Irish Republican Brotherhood, 1858–1924* (Dublin, 1976) and Owen McGee's *The IRB: the Irish Republican Brotherhood from the Land League to Sinn Féin* (Dublin, 2005) are complemented by more cerebral treatments by Garvin and Hutchinson, who examine the causal and motivational forces.[7] The early history of Sinn Féin is important, as there was a presence in Swords from as early as 1906. Michael Laffan, in *The resurrection of Ireland: the Sinn Féin Party, 1916–1923* (Cambridge, 1999), and Brian Feeney, in *Sinn Féin: a hundred turbulent years* (Dublin, 2002), detail this development. P.J. Mathews' *Revival: the Abbey Theatre, Sinn Féin, the Gaelic League and the co-operative movement* (Cork, 2003) develops the links between the different elements that together formed the wider Irish Ireland and self-help identity. There are also a number of key articles relating to aspects of the development of the GAA and Gaelic League.

The historiography only very occasionally references Fingal history, which emphasizes the gap in research that this book addresses. The objective is to contribute to a greater understanding of the progress and achievements of the period, but also the missed opportunities. Rural Fingal was far enough away from life in Dublin city not to be part of the life of the capital, but close enough for the dynamic spirit of the city to influence its politics and culture – yet not close enough to the rest of rural Ireland to be part of the rest of the country. These circumstances make this region a unique area for study.

While the chapters in this book focus on successive chronological periods characterized by events in the national narrative, each is almost a representative case study of the changing fortunes of one type of elite. Hence, the first chapter relates the declining influence of the old ascendancy elite, the second deals with the assumption of local power and influence by the constitutional nationalist elite, and the third looks at the appearance of an alternative in Sinn Féin and a revitalized Irish Republican Brotherhood (IRB). Colonel Joseph Lawless, who fought at the Battle of Ashbourne, writing in late 1954, in his Bureau of Military History witness statement, captured a sense of these changing times prior to the 1916 Rising, and the influence they had on those pivotal events:

> It is not easy for the younger generation to visualise what life was like and the general condition of things in Ireland in the latter part of 1915. Historical writers naturally concentrate upon the highlights and the important events. They often fail to convey a clear impression, because the sidelights and minor incidents which form the background are missing. It was in the arena of local politics that the direct fight was knit at this period.[8]

I believe this is the first such study undertaken of Fingal, and hope it can take its place on the bookshelf beside some notable similar works. These include Michael Wheatley, *Nationalism and the Irish party: provincial Ireland, 1910–16*; Fergus Campbell, *Land and revolution: nationalist politics in the West of Ireland, 1891–1921*; and Donnacha Sean Lucey, 'Land and popular politics in County Kerry, 1872–86'.[9]

1. Fin de siècle, 1891–8

The last decade of the 19th century saw not only the rupture of the nationalist movement in Ireland, split over Parnell's involvement in the O'Shea divorce case and the resultant questioning of his leadership, but also an increasing entrenchment of the emerging nationalist and threatened unionist elites, heightened by agrarian agitation and successive home rule crises. With continuing change brought about by the economic, social and electoral reforms of constructive unionism, the erosion of the position of the landed elite was underway, and an emerging nationalist elite was competing for representation and influence on local administrative bodies. Land ownership was wealth, wealth brought local status and political control, but changing land ownership, growing merchant wealth, and the search for cultural and political identity, would change the balance of elites in Fingal, as throughout Ireland. Long-held suspicions, fears, and animosities occasionally rose to the surface as this entrenchment manifested itself in the local political elites, through their engagement and conduct in these fora. The daily lives, welfare and outlook of the population were influenced by the elite position of landowners, merchants and employers, by their philanthropy and public service, their involvement in local administrative or institutional bodies, and their roles in local cultural and leisure activities. This chapter will focus on those who were involved across several of these spheres, on the spectrum from material to intellectual influence.

The historical area of Fingal, which derives its name from the 'white' or 'fair-haired' foreigners of Viking times, was granted by Henry II to Hugh de Lacy, lord of Meath, and divided into the baronies of Balrothery, Castleknock, Coolock and Nethercross.[1] Roughly correlating to the administrative county of Fingal as now constituted, a substantial portion of the southern parts of the old Coolock barony are now part of Dublin city. The ancient district of 'Fingall', Patrick Archer tells us, 'comprises the major portion of that part of Co. Dublin, which lies north of the river Tolka, and is, according to the Annals of the Four Masters, bordered to the north by the river Delvin'.[2]

Comprising an area of just over 120,000 acres, the 1891 census showed the population numbered 75,694.[3] Of 9,685 individuals in the Balrothery poor law union area over 20 years of age, 36 per cent were listed as 'not returned for employment', so one can assume that they were mostly working in the home, not employed but not in the workhouse, while 26 per cent were engaged directly in agriculture, and 9 per cent were working in domestic service. Agricultural statistics show 33.6 per cent of the land was under crops, and 58.5 per cent

1. Baronies of Co. Dublin, 1900 (reproduced from Patrick Weston Joyce, *Atlas and cyclopedia of Ireland, 1900*)

was grass or grazing land.[4] The economy was almost exclusively agricultural, with 2,565 holdings, almost half of which were less than five acres in size. The main urban centre was Balbriggan, with a population of 2,273, which was the only town with any industry. A small but busy fishing and commercial port exporting corn, meal and flour and importing coal, Balbriggan had a number of renowned hosiery factories – Smyth's, for example, supplied undergarments to Queen Victoria[5] – as well as mills and a salt works.

In 1891, the Co. Dublin grand jury held administrative responsibility for the whole county (excluding Dublin city), across six poor law unions, each with dispensary and local subcommittees, in addition to the local magistracy. In the north county, Balrothery poor law union included the district electoral divisions of Balbriggan, Ballyboghill, Balscaddan, Clonmethon, Donabate, Hollywood, Holmpatrick, Kilsallaghan, Kinsealy (Kinsaley), Lusk, Malahide and Swords. North Dublin union included Howth, Blanchardstown, Castleknock, Clontarf, Coolock, Drumcondra, Finglas and Glasnevin, as well as the part of Dublin city north of the river Liffey. Celbridge poor law union included Clonsilla and Lucan. Dunshaughlin poor law union included Garristown. Virginia Crossman described the function and interrelationships of the different levels of local government in 19th-century Ireland, their evolution and expanding responsibilities, and how the balance of power changed towards the end of the century.[6] The proximity of Fingal to Dublin city and its origins in the 'Pale' may have made this transition slower and somewhat later there, as the proceedings of these bodies illustrate.

Local affairs in Ireland took place against the backdrop of national politics. Catholic tenants paid the bulk of county rates, but administrative power remained largely in the hands of the Protestant landowning class. Landed estates, according to W.E. Vaughan, were 'the great centres of social, economic, and political power, providing employment, capital for improvements and political patronage',[7] thus defining the key features and attributes of this elite group. Terence Dooley defined the gentry as occupants of big-house residences with accompanying estates of 500 acres, and/or as resident members of the local magistracy.[8] He refers to these justices of the peace as the 'established, potentially active gentry in the county', and this class dominated the local elite in Fingal, exercising almost feudal control, to paraphrase Michael Davitt,[9] over both tenants and employees. They were a class Fergus Campbell described as a 'closed elite group'.[10] Some individuals inherited as titled landowners from Anglo-Norman times, like the earl of Howth and Lord Talbot de Malahide, who in 1883 owned 7,377 and 1,893 acres, respectively, in Co. Dublin, where they were resident. In addition, the earl of Howth owned 2,061 acres in Co. Meath and Talbot held 1,680 acres in Cos Cavan and Westmeath.[11] The Dublin estates of Charles Cobbe, at Newbridge House, Donabate, comprised 9,948 acres, while Sir Roger Palmer held 3,991 acres at his seat at Kenure Park, Rush, out of a total landholding of 98,954 acres, with estates in Cos Mayo and Sligo, and in Britain. In 1891, these individuals, significant economic players, were only peripherally involved in Fingal local politics. Cobbe died in 1886, the others concentrated on the management of their estates, or were involved elsewhere in national or ceremonial duties that excluded extensive local participation.[12]

Two landed families, Taylor and Hamilton, dominated parliamentary representation in the two-seat Dublin County constituency throughout the 19th century. The constituency returned Conservative MPs Thomas Edward Taylor of Ardgillan, Balbriggan, from 1841 until his death in 1883, and the father and son, James Hans Hamilton of Sheepmore, Blanchardstown, from 1841 to 1863, and Ion Trant Hamilton, later Lord Holmpatrick of Abbottstown, Castleknock, who sat as an MP from 1863 to 1885. Ion Trant Hamilton's grandfather, and James Hans' father, James, had previously served in the old Irish parliament in Dublin from 1798 to 1800 and at Westminster from 1801 to 1822. Taylor defeated the emerging home rule politician Charles Stewart Parnell for one of the Co. Dublin seats in 1874, having served as government chief whip from 1866, and been appointed a privy counsellor in 1868. He was appointed chancellor of the duchy of Lancaster in 1874. Parnell would be successful at the polls a year later, when he was elected as the member for Co. Meath in 1875.[13] A close confidant of Parnell, Fingal tenant farmer and Land League organizer Andrew Kettle, described Taylor and Hamilton as 'the leaders of the "Dublin Six",[14] men who had the reputation of being intolerant religious bigots and bad landlords'. The term 'Dublin Six' referred to the six conservative MPs who represented Dublin city and county in the 1850s and 1860s, and espoused English Tory and Orange policies rather than representing Dublin. Kettle had been exhorting Parnell to run against Taylor and Hamilton in Co. Dublin from before the 1874 general election.[15] When the single-seat Dublin County North constituency was introduced in 1885, the nationalist and home rule candidate J.J. Clancy was returned. Clancy was a journalist and career politician from Co. Galway who did not reside in Fingal but in Kingstown, and was not involved in any local bodies. He was, however, a close colleague of Andrew Kettle, and held the seat continuously until 1918, when he lost to the local Sinn Féin candidate.[16] In 1891, the Dublin County North electorate stood at only 11,743 for a population of 75,009,[17] indicating the level of parliamentary franchise.

With his pedigree, Ion Trant Hamilton, deputy lieutenant (DL) of Co. Dublin[18] and justice of the peace (JP), was effectively the leader of the conservative and unionist elite in Fingal, if not Dublin. He was vice president of the Unionist Alliance Fund, chair of the Dublin branch of the Irish Landowners Convention, president of the Irish Loyal and Patriotic Union, and the main driving force behind the election of the unionist Sir Horace Plunkett in Dublin County South in 1892.[19] Plunkett was the third son of Lord Dunsany, and had returned from a career as a rancher in the United States on the death of his father in 1889. He would go on to play a founding role in the development of the co-operative farm movement in Ireland. Landlord brothers Edward Hamilton Woods, DL, of Milverton House, Skerries, and Warren St Leger Woods, of Whitestown, Balbriggan, both of whom were magistrates and poor law guardians (PLGs), were nephews of Thomas Taylor of Ardgillan through their mother, and second cousins of Ion Trant through their grandmother Sarah. Henry Alexander Hamilton, DL, JP, PLG, of Hampton Hall, Balbriggan, a land agent, from a landowning family, was also related to Ion Trant Hamilton, with both families tracing their ancestry back to James Hamilton, first earl of

2. Ion Trant Hamilton, Lord Holmpatrick

Clandeboye. All served as Co. Dublin grand jurors in the 1890s, and were board members of Richmond Lunatic Asylum and members of the Sackville Street Club. They all qualified as *ex officio* guardians of Balrothery poor law union, appointed as major ratepayers rather than through election, and often had multiple voting rights based on property ownership. They were all involved in the Church of Ireland as select vestrymen, and Henry A. Hamilton was a representative to the Dublin Diocesan Synod and Dublin Diocesan Council, and a member of the Representative Church Body.[20]

A significant landowner with 3,647 acres in Dublin at Castleknock and at Holmpatrick, Skerries, Ion Trant Hamilton owned 3,242 acres in Cos Laois, Down and Meath, and was married to Victoria Wellesley, a granddaughter of the duke of Wellington, who was dame president of the Primrose League, a conservative women's organization.[21] Appointed lord lieutenant of Co. Dublin in 1892, he was a privy counsellor and chairman of the Co. Dublin grand jury until a year before his death in 1898. Conservative unionists dominated the 23-man Co. Dublin grand jury, which met annually over a three- to four-day session, but conducted most of its business through committees during the year. At the 1891 session, 20 of the members were identifiable as conservative unionists, based on their attendance at the unionist convention for Leinster, Munster and Connacht in Dublin in June 1892.[22] The other three were Catholic businessmen. Anthony O'Neill and Edward Fottrell, liberal unionists, had notably supported the English liberal unionist Lord Hartington in Dublin in 1887. O'Neill, a Dublin-based coachbuilder, held the lucrative mail-delivery contract for the post office, and was an omnibus proprietor, a poor law guardian of the North Dublin union and an auditor of the Midland and Great Western Railway. Fottrell was chair of the Alliance and Dublin Consumers' Gas Company, more commonly known as the Dublin Gas Company. James Milo Burke, the vice chairman of the Rathdown poor law union, was a barrister and landowner, and signed the Roman Catholic petition against home rule in 1893.[23] Anthony Strong Hussey, a Catholic magistrate and poor law guardian, owned 600 acres in north Co. Dublin and 4,700 in Co. Meath, but lived in Fingal, with a residence at Westown, Naul; he served on the grand jury twice, in 1891 and 1896.[24] The grand jury conducted its business largely in agreement and without fuss. Its members demonstrated their political affiliation in 1893, during the home rule bill readings, by passing a motion expressing 'undiminished loyalty to HM the Queen', and recording their:

> unanimous opinion that any measure whatever tending to weaken the legislative union now existing between Great Britain and Ireland would be most disastrous to both countries and certain to affect most injuriously the interests and imperil the safety of the Empire.

This motion was proposed by Colonel Gore Lindsay (Glasnevin), seconded by Thomas L. Plunkett (Portmarnock), and approved by I.T. Hamilton.[25]

Balrothery poor law union represented the bulk of the area of Fingal, and lay wholly within the rural north of Co. Dublin. The Balbriggan town commissioners were responsible for their own urban area, and the North Dublin union had responsibility for an area that included the urban north of Dublin city. Thus, the dynamics of local politics within the Fingal elite is best examined by confining the study primarily to the activities of Balrothery poor law guardians.[26] Over the period 1891 to 1898, prior to the formation of Dublin county council, which took over many of its duties, newspaper reports of the weekly minutes list over 130 men who attended meetings of the board of poor law guardians, its local subcommittees or dispensary committees. The chairman was usually from a Catholic farming background, the vice and deputy-vice chairmen were unionists, and the most consistent attendees were unionists. Thomas McCourt, Lanestown, until his death in 1892, and then William Boylan, Jordanstown, Holmpatrick, occupied the chair throughout these years. Justices of the peace Mark Perrin, Arthur Maxwell and Alexander Sharpe Deane, and Catholic JPs A.S. Hussey, Patrick Thunder and Colonel James

FitzEustace Forster, all landowners, together with Balbriggan coal merchant T.W. Hamlet, attended the most meetings during this period.[27] Perrin, of Beau, Lusk, was a retired barrister and registrar of judgments; he was a son of Louis Perrin, a Whig MP in the 1830s who had supported Catholic emancipation and was critical of grand jury corruption and jobbery, speaking out in the House of Commons. Deane was a retired land commission official. Hamlet was barony cess collector for the Co. Dublin grand jury for the district of Balrothery East, the area around the town of Balbriggan. These magistrates, with roles on the bench as well as in local government, had considerable influence over the everyday affairs in the locality.[28] Perrin, Hamlet and Hussey were the most prominent at meetings, with many debates or arguments occurring among themselves, rather than arising from political divisions.[29] For example, in July 1893, the *Drogheda Independent* reported an ongoing argument that carried on for a number of weeks, in which T.W. Hamlet complained of the absence of a resident magistrate in Balbriggan, where Hussey attended as a magistrate.

With most meetings poorly attended, these unionist voices were thus the dominant ones. This was clearly a case of a group exercising influence without necessarily occupying the top position. Thomas McCourt and William Boylan fulfilled a neutral rather than leadership role as chairmen. The Woods brothers, as busy magistrates and grand jurors, were less regular attendees, but prominent at crucial times and they sat on a number of special and local committees. Much work was delegated to local and dispensary committees, and it was at this level that farmer and merchant representation was strongest. Patrick Kettle, Nicholas Long and Joseph Lawless of Swords, and Patrick McCabe of Balbriggan, pursued a nationalist, tenant farmer agenda. Major landowning *ex officio* members – such as Talbot de Malahide, Hamilton (Palmer), Thomas Plunkett (Portmarnock), Thomas and Robert Aungier (Swords) and Matthew Corbally (Rathbeale Hall, Swords) – rarely attended, or turned up only for votes on tenders or appointments. For example, there was high attendance on 26 November 1892, when Mr Tolan was elected rate collector after four weeks of tied or near-tied votes. Plunkett and Corbally were deputy lieutenants of the county and with Thomas Aungier were members of the grand jury. Robert Aungier was a magistrate. All were significant landowners.[30] Andrew Kettle, although the senior nationalist political personality, confined his involvement to the local committee for Malahide, where he lived. Responsibilities of the guardians included the running of the workhouse, outdoor poor relief, sanitation and dispensary provision, with the unionist members anxious to keep matters apolitical and 'within the rules'. Increasingly, motions of a political nature received in correspondence from other unions seeking support, such as those from sister unions in Lismore and Limerick calling for an amnesty for Fenian political prisoners, would highlight the underlying political differences in the membership. Some members, such as A.S. Deane, wanted to be completely apolitical, dealing with only matters pertinent to the ratepayers, while Hussey

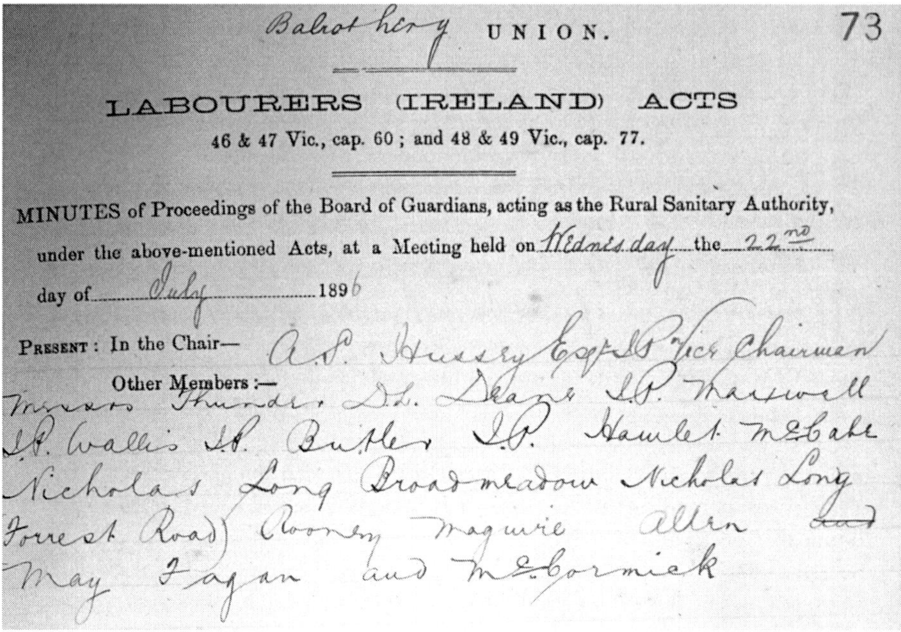

Balrothery UNION. 73

LABOURERS (IRELAND) ACTS

46 & 47 Vic., cap. 60 ; and 48 & 49 Vic., cap. 77.

MINUTES of Proceedings of the Board of Guardians, acting as the Rural Sanitary Authority, under the above-mentioned Acts, at a Meeting held on Wednesday the 22nd day of July 1896

PRESENT: In the Chair— A.S. Hussey Esq J.P. Vice Chairman

Other Members:— Messrs Thunder D.L. Deane J.P. Maxwell J.P. Wallis J.P. Butler J.P. Hamlet McCabe Nicholas Long Broadmeadow Nicholas Long (Forrest Road) Rooney Maguire Allen May Fagan and McCormick

3. Attendance at a meeting of the board of Balrothery poor law guardians on 22 July 1896 (courtesy of Fingal Local Studies and County Archives)

mischievously wondered why Balrothery did not send motions out on their own behalf of a different nature. This highlighted the truth that Balrothery guardians at this stage were somewhat less nationalist in their constitution than those in parts of the country more remote from the capital.[31] In 1898, when the union was invited to take part in the Wolfe Tone centenary commemoration in Dublin, Hussey and Perrin would not consent, but Charles Gallen, a factory owner from Balbriggan, was enthusiastic and won the day. A delegation was sent, signalling a shift in power and priorities before the imminent introduction of the Local Government Act.[32]

When the Irish National Federation was founded in Dublin in March 1891, calling for Parnell's resignation, two Fingal priests – Revd Waters of Balbriggan and Revd Carrick of St Margaret's – attended, along with five members of the Rush branch. The Balbriggan branch held its first meeting in June, with mill owner Charles Gallen and Patrick McCabe, both poor law guardians, prominent.[33] When the Balrothery board of guardians met later that month, James Ennis proposed and Patrick Kettle seconded that the guardians sign a welcome address to Parnell, who was due to visit Balbriggan the following week. All supported the motion except Mark Perrin and James Rooney. An address was duly given when Parnell arrived by special train from Dublin for the visit, accompanied by local MP Clancy, Andrew Kettle and John Redmond. The Balbriggan branch of the Irish National Federation became increasingly anti-Redmond, and in 1892 it opposed his support of the land purchase and local government bills, declaring them 'sham' and 'worthless' measures, and ridiculing Parnell as 'a moral leper, loathsome to all pure minded men, an obstacle to the cause he had hitherto been honoured leader'. They supported Joseph Mooney's candidature against sitting MP Clancy, but Mooney's election meetings in Swords, Donabate and Skerries were disrupted by the Redmond-Clancyite faction. A number of poor law guardians were present or allegedly involved, and Andrew Kettle was alleged to have been behind the disruption. Edward Hamilton Woods ran as a unionist candidate, expecting to profit from the nationalist split, but was beaten into third place, as Clancy retained the seat.[34] While the general depression in agriculture in the early 1890s exercised the attention of the Balrothery board of guardians, who noted in September 1892 the prevailing environment of 'unsaleable cattle, poor harvest prospects, and called for rent reductions from landlords', the *Drogheda Independent*'s editor was not convinced of the sincerity of Redmond or his supporters, and wrote, a month later: 'The interest shown at present in the cause of the evicted tenants of Ireland by the Redmondite faction is very laudable, if it were only honest.'[35]

The Gaelic Athletic Association officially supported Parnell after the split, and suffered falling membership and disaffiliating clubs in the early 1890s. Clubs and county boards split into clerical and Fenian factions, the number of clubs falling from 1,000 in 1890 to 220 in 1892. Adverse economic conditions contributed, as did the decision of the Dublin county board not to affiliate in 1893–4.[36] Emigration affected the organization in rural Ireland, but in Fingal the population increased by 3 per cent in this period.[37] The GAA remained diminished throughout the remainder of the decade, with little popular enthusiasm and few resources, having accumulated debts from the 'American Invasion' promotional tour to the US in 1889.[38] By 1896, there were only eight clubs in Fingal affiliated to the Dublin county board: Balscadden Blues, Fearnots and Magh go Bragh (all Balbriggan); Fingallians of Swords; Innisfails of St Doulagh's in Coolock; Sarsfields of Lucan; Hugh O'Neills of Glasnevin; and the Parnell Volunteers in the north city. In 1888, there had been 23. Games were irregular and often played as part of a wider sports event or for fundraising purposes.[39] Although it was founded in Dublin in 1893, there is little evidence of any penetration of the Gaelic League into the rural north of the county during the years up to 1898. Séamus Ó Maitiú mentions a branch in Naul in 1899, but contends that the Gaelic League really only took hold following the renewed popular nationalist enthusiasm around opposition to the Boer War and the 1798 commemorations.[40] The setting up of dual Gaelic League-GAA clubs, such as the Keating branch in Dublin, invigorated both organizations, and attracted IRB members such as Cathal Brugha.[41] Police intelligence reports regularly refer to matters in the county as 'quiet and peaceable', adding in June 1898 that 'farmers seem to take very little interest in politics'. This sentiment is very common in the Co. Dublin RIC inspector's monthly confidential reports.[42]

Throughout the decade, tenant representatives continued to pursue rent reductions, through the land commission courts, and from the landlords with whom they were sharing board and committee meetings. The Land Law (Ireland) Act 1881 (44 & 45 Vic. c. 49) conceded the 'three Fs' of fair rent, free sale and fixity of tenure, with 75 per cent funding of tenant purchase available from the government, repayable at 5 per cent over 35 years. Tenants could secure 15-year tenure at a fair agreed rent with the landlord, or a binding judicial rent at court.[43] Patrick Kettle had rent on a tenancy from Col. Forster reduced from £186 4*s*. 4*d*. to £56 at the land commission court in August 1892.[44] In March 1897, Balbriggan town commissioner Andrew Derham had rents reduced by in excess of £65 on eight tenancies of approximately 36 acres from his landlord Ion Trant Hamilton, all in Skerries.[45] There were very few cases of tenants purchasing their holdings in this period, the extended Kettle family being the exception when Patrick, John and Margaret Kettle bought 131 acres from Col. Forster in 1895.[46] That same year, the Balrothery poor law guardians and MP Clancy jointly brought a case under the Representation of the People Act against Sir Roger Palmer to answer 286 complaints of failing to complete and return forms of requisition, which would have affected franchise entitlements of his tenants. Palmer was a veteran of the Crimean War, took part in the Charge of the Light Brigade, and had a reputation as a harsh landlord, particularly in his estates in the west of Ireland.[47]

Ion Trant Hamilton, now Lord Holmpatrick, died in 1898, aged 58 years, with one obituary in the *Kildare Observer* describing him as an 'uncompromising conservative'.[48] The *London Times*, not unexpectedly, praised him as a 'staunch Conservative', who was:

> always tolerant of the opinions of those whose principles were not in harmony with his own. His speeches were cast in a practical mould, and they never disclosed anything like a rancorous spirit. In social life he was deservedly esteemed by all classes. His sympathy with objects of charity assumed on all appropriate occasions a practical form, and in contributing financial aid he refused to be fettered by considerations of party or creed.[49]

He was like many of his class and generation who were uncompromising in the defence of their own rights and privileges yet could be generous thereafter in philanthropic and charitable causes. As the end of the decade approached, the system of patronage and privilege, which he and his class had embraced, perpetuated and fought to maintain, locally and nationally, was crumbling. The end of the century was echoing the end of an era for his social and political class. The next decade would show whether this decline in fortunes was terminal.

2. Energy and purpose, 1899–1909

Described by Michael Davitt as the 'greatest of all victories won by Irish forces', the Local Government (Ireland) Act 1898 (61 & 62 Vic., c. 37), was passed in August 1898.[1] It introduced to Fingal a two-tier system of local administration, with a single elected Dublin county council covering the county area outside of the Dublin corporation city boundaries, and the elected rural district councils of Balrothery, North Dublin and Celbridge No. 2 covering the north of the county. Balbriggan town council remained as a borough council, and Garristown district electoral division, or dispensary area, was transferred from the Dunshaughlin poor law union into Balrothery rural district council and Dublin county council administration. The grand jury remained, but with mainly legal responsibilities, while the poor law boards of guardians became subordinate to the appropriate county or district councils. The increased enfranchisement and additional devolved powers would contribute to a political transformation that would start to democratize municipal administration. Political brokerage, patronage and representation for the nationalist electorate were now possible. Universal education and increased literacy would lead to a political awakening and introduce political alternatives for the first time. The fledgling organizations of labour and advanced nationalism could challenge the incumbent elites, if not displace them, and could gain the opportunity to promote an alternative message.[2] Regardless of the extent of the powers granted, this presented the opportunity to prove that the Irish could successfully govern themselves. Although the Irish Parliamentary Party had not actively campaigned for the introduction of the Local Government Act, J.J. Clancy published an extensive guide to it, with the grandiose and verbose title:

> A handbook of local government in Ireland [containing an explanatory introduction to the Local Government (Ireland) Act, 1898 together with the text of the act, the orders in Council, and the rules made thereunder relating to county council, rural district council, and guardian's elections] with an index

This gave the impression of his approbation.[3] Redmond claimed that it 'disestablished the old ascendancy class from its position of power and made the mass of the Irish people masters of all the finance and all of the local affairs of Ireland'.[4] It was a major step in franchise reform in Ireland, giving the vote in local elections to men over the age of 21, and women over the age of 30,

4. Andrew Kettle, aged 75 years

who were householders or occupiers in dwellings of over £4 rateable valuation. Ratepayers and freemen continued their existing entitlements, including multiple voting based on property rights. This created greater electoral accountability, forcing the political elite to take cognizance of an electorate previously ignored or paid only lip service.[5]

As 1898 ended, the aspirant political elite in Fingal prepared for the forthcoming local government elections. A meeting of leading nationalist electors at the Metropole Hotel in Dublin discussed how to secure the maximum return of nationalists to Dublin county council. In attendance were members of three families that would figure prominently in the political life of Fingal over the next 20 years: the O'Neills, the Kettles and Lawlesses.[6] The O'Neill family at Kinsealy and the Kettle family, with farms at Malahide, Coolock, Swords and St Margaret's, as well as their close supporters, would dominate the influential positions on local bodies, and on political, cultural and farmers' organizations. Patrick Joseph (P.J.) and Joseph O'Neill were cousins who lived on adjoining farms, originally of about 160 acres each, and built up their holdings and political bases in the immediate area.[7] Their fathers had been involved with the repeal movement.[8] They were distant relations of city councillor Laurence O'Neill, who owned a farm locally, but worked mainly as a potato factor in

Dublin, with whom the O'Neills and Kettles had extensive business dealings.[9] He would become lord mayor of Dublin in 1917.[10]

Andrew Kettle was born in 1833 into a prosperous farming family with links back to the United Irishmen. Having lived through the repeal movement and the Famine, he took an interest in politics, and while developing his farming interests was instrumental in setting up the Dublin Tenants' Defence Association in 1873, alongside the O'Neills and his father-in-law Laurence McCourt. He secured the support of Cardinal Cullen to back Parnell to run in North Dublin in the election of 1874 against the 'bigoted' sitting MPs.[11] Parnell was defeated, but won the Meath by-election the following year. An associate of Isaac Butt, Kettle was close to both Davitt and Parnell in the land struggle, and served as honorary secretary of the Land League.[12] His farm at Millview, Malahide, was used to test the fair-rents provisions of the 1881 Land Act, against landlord Talbot de Malahide.[13] Davitt described him as:

> one of the most loyal, energetic and able advocates given by the gentleman farmer class of Ireland to the cause of tenant right and nationalism, from 1848 to the present time. He was both a friend and lieutenant to every leader of the people in his long life of most useful service to his country, and was honoured by each and all of them as his sterling qualities and conspicuous abilities entitled him to be.[14]

When Andrew Kettle was in Kilmainham Gaol with Parnell, local farmers – including Nicholas Long, Peter Early and Joseph Lawless – banded together to harvest his crop, working at his farms at Drinan, near Swords, and Malahide. Kettle's experience and influence permeates the period, in the background, through to his death in 1916.

The *ex officio* guardians of the Balrothery union and the serving magistrates of the area met at the Gresham Hotel on 12 January 1899 to select candidates to represent the landowning – and by extension unionist – community. Five of the rural district council candidates had been grand jury members, and Edward Hamilton Woods would contest one of the Dublin county council seats. They decided that selection should be on strictly non-political grounds and therefore agreed not to nominate opponents to William Cumisky in Balbriggan, a merchant and the chairman of the Balbriggan town commissioners, or Thomas Aungier in Swords, a Catholic JP, landowner and outgoing grand juror.[15] Aungier wrote to electors, through the *Drogheda Independent*, citing labourers' housing as an issue he wished to address, having aligned himself with Thomas McLean, secretary of the Swords Labourers' District Defence Association. He was criticized at an election meeting by P.J. O'Neill, who had strong Irish Parliamentary Party backing, as a unionist now trying to reinvent himself as a nationalist with a newfound concern for labourers. He maintained it was tillage farmers, like himself and Andrew Kettle, who provided employment for the labouring class, adding that he had worked for many years with the MP J.J. Clancy to secure the franchise for labourers. Aungier and his labourer supporters were critical of O'Neill's personal ambition, his treatment of his workers, and his outside backing from national politicians. At a meeting at Lusk to select candidates, the local parish priest, Revd Heffernan, in the chair, took the opportunity to condemn the grand jury system and its sectarian unionist bias, dismissing those former members of the grand jury now seeking council seats.[16]

The local election results produced what Pauric Travers called 'a bloodless revolution'.[17] From outnumbering nationalists on grand juries 15:1, unionists now found themselves outnumbered by nationalists on county councils 3:1. From even representation as poor law guardians, they were now outnumbered 4:1.[18] Matthew Potter describes the 'displacement of old gentry by the new bourgeoisie of farmers and shopkeepers as representing a continuation of the trend whereby the "shopocracy" had already taken control of town councils and boards of guardians'.[19] Prior to the elections, Balbriggan town council was the only body in Fingal where any major shift had occurred.[20] Of 33 successful candidates elected to Balrothery rural district council, only four were affirmed unionists, all prominent poor law guardians and magistrates. A further three were co-opted, including Thomas Aungier and E.H. Woods. District councillors automatically became poor law guardians, and the members wanted to retain the experience and commitment of those who had served well in the past. P.J. O'Neill was elected chairman, and the new council took the opportunity to pass a motion supporting home rule, with two votes of dissent, both Catholic unionists, A.S. Hussey and Col. Forster.[21] Balrothery RDC area elected three nationalists to Dublin county council: William Cumisky, Balbriggan, unopposed; Edward Rooney, Lusk, who defeated Woods with over 80 per cent of the vote; and P.J. O'Neill, Swords, who defeated Aungier with only 55 per cent of the votes cast.[22] The closeness of this contest indicates that despite the heavyweight support for O'Neill, there was strong local support for Aungier and some distrust of O'Neill. Still, he became the first chairman of Dublin county council in 1899, a position he held for the next 20 years in addition to being chairman of Balrothery RDC.[23] His cousin Joseph O'Neill became chairman of North Dublin RDC.[24]

The first meeting of Dublin county council took place in Kilmainham Courthouse, symbolically in the grand jury room, on 2 May 1899. Less than one-third of the 29 attendees were unionists. In addition to those elected representatives from Balrothery, Charles Gallen and Joseph O'Neill were *ex officio* representatives of Balrothery and North Dublin rural district councils, Joseph Mooney (Castleknock), J.J. Flood (Coolock) and James McKenna (Howth) making up the group from the Fingal districts. Anthony S. Hussey, Naul, was a grand jury nominee, bringing the representation from Fingal to nine. The council's first resolution recorded:

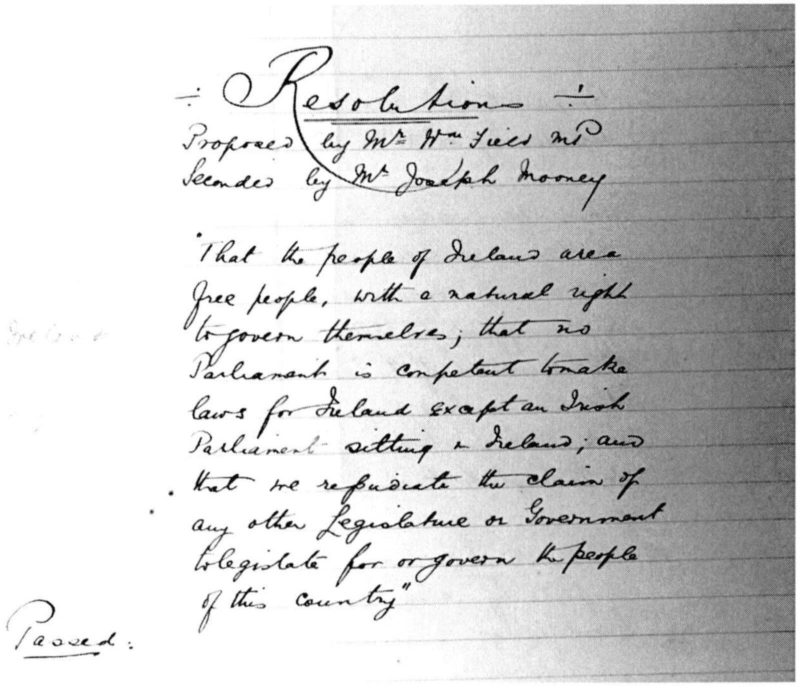

÷ Resolution ÷
Proposed by Mr Wm Field MP
Seconded by Mr Joseph Mooney

"That the people of Ireland are a free people, with a natural right to govern themselves; that no Parliament is competent to make laws for Ireland except an Irish Parliament sitting in Ireland; and that we repudiate the claim of any other Legislature or Government to legislate for or govern the people of this country"

Passed:

5. First resolution passed at the first meeting of Dublin county council, May 1899 (courtesy of Fingal Local Studies and County Archives)

> That the people of Ireland are a free people with a national right to govern themselves; that no Parliament is competent to make laws for Ireland except an Irish Parliament sitting in Ireland; and that we repudiate the claim of any other Legislature or Government to legislate for or govern the people of this country.[25]

Additional motions called for a Catholic university, tenants' rights, land purchase, the release of political prisoners and supports for agricultural and industrial development, as the new council sought to send a message of its nationalist intentions to the establishment. However, the minutes show that the council quickly settled down to the work in hand in its first year, with various committees performing effectively. The council met 42 times in its first year, in addition to committee meetings, with chairman P.J. O'Neill (37 attendances), Mooney, (38), Cumisky (37), Joseph O'Neill (35), Flood (34) and Gallen (30) among the best attendees. It is notable that the unionist nominees were not among these. Average attendance was just under 18 meetings.[26]

The next decade would see some of these prominent councillors become conspicuous at the various national conventions of the United Irish League. The

UIL had been founded in January 1898 by the disillusioned former nationalist MP William O'Brien, who was dissatisfied with party factions and infighting in the years following the Parnell split. He sought to refocus on land reform for small tenant farmers, targeting large graziers and ranchers and seeking land redistribution. As the UIL rapidly expanded, it became a threat to and then became the de facto grassroots support base for the Irish Parliamentary Party. Dominated by the local tenant farmer elites, it would provide a vehicle for exerting local influence and control in matters concerning land reform, local administration and the harnessing of support for home rule. Despite close working relationships on local matters, national politics was never far from the surface. When two unionist members proposed a vote of sympathy to the royal family on the death of Queen Victoria, nationalist members added the amendment:

> that sympathising with the Royal Family on the death of Her Majesty in no way admits that Irishmen are at all satisfied with the treatment accorded to their country by the government of England.[27]

The biggest issue facing the council in its first three-year term was attempts by Dublin corporation to annex portions of the more lucrative taxation districts of the townships and rural districts close to the city, such as Glasnevin. In 1900, when the Dublin Boundaries Act brought Kilmainham and Drumcondra into the city, the unionist councils and ratepayers of the independent townships of Pembroke, Rathmines and Clontarf, which were part of Dublin county council, grew anxious at the prospect of their annexation by the corporation.[28] Nationalists were becoming more organized through the United Irish League, agitating for further agrarian reforms and home rule. When the Irish Parliamentary Party reunited in 1900 under Redmond, the potential existed for a coherent political mass movement to press for further progressive legislation and, ultimately, home rule. Queen Victoria's visit to Ireland in April 1900 and the ongoing Boer War provided opportunities to harness nationalist public feeling, reflected in a series of motions passed at local council level.[29] P.J. O'Neill and Thomas Luke Plunkett, who lived quite near each other, exchanged critical correspondence in the press over the latter's exhortation of his fellow Catholics to welcome the visit.[30]

Following the passing of the Irish Land Act, 1903 (3 Edw. VII, c. 37), known as the Wyndham Act, Clancy and O'Neill encouraged tenants to organize themselves and approach their landlords with a view to negotiating the purchase of their holdings.[31] Earlier legislation gave Irish tenants adequate protection but failed to quell demands for land reform, in reality the transfer of ownership to the tenants. Despite a succession of land purchase acts, less than one in seven of 545,000 occupiers had acquired their holdings prior to 1903. The fixing of judicial rents downwards by the courts meant it made no sense for tenants to purchase at the prices sought by landlords. Wyndham addressed these anomalies, ensuring that the landowner got a good price while the tenant effectively took a 20-year mortgage to pay for it, at a price lower than the previous fixed rent. Within five years, almost half of all tenant farmers were able to buy their holdings with British government loans.[32] The partial settlement of the land question only opened the way for increased demands for home rule, the opposite of what the government had hoped to achieve by granting concessions. Land purchase grants enabled the political elite to add to their wealth. P.J. and John Kettle acquired 138 acres from the Buchan-Sydserff sale, near Swords, where they held tenancies, in 1908, with district councillors Nicholas Long and Patrick Cuffe also purchasing. When 810 acres from the nearby McDonnel-Slade estate was sold in October 1909, the purchasers included Frank Lawless' mother, who bought the family farm of 209 acres. Frank and his sister-in-law purchased the farm his brother Edward (Ned) worked at Balheary. Local landowners the Corbally family acquired over 500 acres. Thomas Aungier secured most of the balance.[33]

District councillor Patrick J. Kettle, son of Patrick and nephew of Andrew Kettle, was a farmer and an independent-minded, enthusiastic nationalist. The United Irish League national conventions held to discuss the political matters of the day regularly had the experienced Andrew Kettle in attendance, ensuring a direct line of communication between the Fingal nationalist elite and the higher echelons of the Irish Parliamentary Party. Both were at a meeting in Swords in May 1900 setting up a branch of the United Irish League. P.J. Kettle became president, with close supporter and neighbour Frank Lawless as vice president and Nicholas Long as treasurer. A vacancy saw Lawless co-opted onto Balrothery rural district council in February 1901.[34] Andrew Kettle chaired the inaugural meeting of the North Dublin executive of the United Irish League in 1902, while P.J. and Andrew's son Thomas were elected treasurer and secretary, respectively.[35] Thomas (Tom) Kettle was a student at University College Dublin at this time, where he was close to both James Joyce and Oliver St John Gogarty. He would soon become president of the famed Young Ireland branch of the United Irish League, with contemporaries like future suffragist and pacifist Francis Sheehy-Skeffington.

P.J. Kettle and Lawless worked closely in developing the Gaelic League in Swords, and throughout Fingal. Lawless was also president of Fingallians GAA club.[36] In December 1903, leading IRB figures P.T. Daly and James Egan spoke at a Gaelic League meeting in Swords on 'the life and works of Thomas Davis' to attendees from other branches and GAA clubs across the county and city. Daly was a prolific speaker, energetic IRB recruiter, and under police surveillance at this time.[37] Other speakers included P.H. Pearse, editor of the Gaelic League newspaper, and Belfast writer Alice Milligan.[38] Talks such as this, and open-air Gaelic cultural festivals, known as *aeríochtaí*, enabled the building up of networks of cultural and nationalist groups, as well as providing leisure and educational events for the wider public. In 1904, one of the founders of the

Gaelic League, Eoin MacNeill, was living at Hazelbrook, Malahide, and served as president of the Fingal Feis committee, alongside P.J. Kettle.[39] By 1909, there were sufficient GAA clubs in Fingal for it to set up its own leagues, independent of the Dublin city leagues – but under Dublin county board administration – in both hurling and football. The following year, they received permission from the county board to start a schools competition.[40]

In 1902, Swords Labourers' Defence Association, led by Thomas McLean, who had supported Aungier in 1899, threatened to run candidates in the local elections. McLean took the district councils to task, and Frank Lawless in particular, alleging favouritism in the allocation of labourers' cottages.[41] Thomas W. Hamlet, long active as a poor law guardian, was elected to Dublin county council in 1902 for Balbriggan, describing himself as a Protestant home ruler. He had been a delegate to the unionist convention in Dublin in 1892. Three county councillors – Gallen, Rooney and Cumisky – declined to run again, citing personal and business pressures.[42]

When the North County Dublin Farmers' Association started in 1905, with P.J. Kettle as president and 53 members, the committee included many United Irish League officers, including Michael Dunne of St Margaret's, and Joseph Christie of Swords. It brought together farmers of different political and religious backgrounds to represent their collective interests, inspired by the success of the Irish Cattle Traders and Owners' Association, headed by the MP for Blackrock, Co. Dublin, city councillor and butcher William Field. As the 1905 local elections approached, the ambitious P.J. Kettle stood against P.J. O'Neill for the Swords seat on the county council, despite his uncle Andrew exhorting him not to. Endorsed by Thomas McLean, he won by 561 votes to 540. P.J. Kettle came from the same area west of Swords as Thomas Aungier, so it is likely that he had the support of the same labourer vote from three years earlier.[43] O'Neill was subsequently co-opted and re-elected chairman and regained his seat in the following election in 1908. This co-option caused some dissension among councillors, who saw it as usurping the electorate. Through 1906, Kettle took up the cause of the labourer, appearing at demonstrations at Oldtown and Swords organized by the Labour League against the allocation of lands to graziers, and calling for one-acre plots for labourers.[44] Calls for town housing reform ran parallel to those for land for the landless labourer. The Labourers (Ireland) Act, 1906 (6 Edw. VII, c. 37), and the Housing of the Working Classes (Ireland) Act, 1908 (8 Edw. VII, c. 61), also known as the Clancy Act, after its sponsor, were modest improvements. Both provided state support in the form of council funding for house construction and rental, and loans for house purchase, similar to the land purchase mechanism available to tenant farmers. MPs Clancy and Field began to attend mass meetings, but by summer of 1907, at a meeting at Malahide, the appearance of Irish Parliamentary Party members on such platforms drew heckling from members of the North Dublin United Labour League, tired of their empty rhetoric. They were denied

6. J.J. Clancy, MP

an opportunity to speak, but the new local Sinn Féin organization intervened on their behalf, holding a rival meeting afterwards. In 1908, Naul Labour Union threw their support behind candidates who espoused the labourers' cause, and helped Andrew Mooney top the poll in Garristown.[45]

Historian F.S.L. Lyons called the period from 1903 to 1907 'the watershed', during which 'matters moved not only sedately, but in a variety of directions that at first sight seem if not random at least to have little obvious connection with each other'. After this period, he contends that 'many paths begin perceptibly to converge' as the 'pace quickens and complexity deepens almost year by year'.[46] The story of Frank Lawless reflects this. A close supporter of P.J. Kettle, Lawless was the chairman of the recently formed local Sinn Féin organization in Swords. His father Joseph was a close supporter of Andrew Kettle and had been a poor law guardian. Frank failed to be elected or co-opted onto the district council in 1905 and would fail at the polls again in 1908 – by only four votes.[47] His nationalism was becoming more militant, as his Irish language promotion efforts demonstrated. In addition to his farm at Saucerstown, he ran a butcher's shop in Swords and was fined for having his name on his delivery cart in Irish only, which was illegal. When he refused to pay the fine, the police confiscated a sofa from his family home to recover the fine by 'distress of goods'. The local

7. Frank Lawless (courtesy of Swords Historical Society)

Drogheda Independent newspaper humorously reported the strenuous efforts of the local constabulary in executing this court order, adding that they were able to rest on the said sofa, at intervals, as they conveyed it back to the court.[48]

The *Sinn Féin Weekly* newspaper reported on a meeting convened with the aim of starting a Sinn Féin branch in Swords in October 1906, chaired by Lawless, with speakers from Dublin including Seán T. O'Kelly, then an elected Sinn Féin city councillor with Dublin corporation, and the Sord Colmcille pipe band parading beforehand, which no doubt aided attendance. At this meeting, Lawless professed:

> I was a member of the Land League and later the United Irish League, but since Parnell's death, every year that passes strengthens my belief that no good can come to this country through parliamentarianism.[49]

He quickly moved on to the Dublin executive of Sinn Féin, representing Swords under his Gaelic name, P.S. Ó Laoidhleas. By 1908, he was on the national executive of Sinn Féin, where records show he was the north Dublin representative, contributing on agricultural matters.[50] Frank's brother James V. Lawless represented the Glasnevin and Drumcondra branch, and was chairman

8. Fingallians GAA football team, 1910. Frank Lawless is first from right back row (courtesy of Swords Historical Society)

of the trade subcommittee of the National Council, promoting Sinn Féin policy to trade unionists. In September 1907, he was appointed assistant secretary of Dublin county council, from 43 applicants, on the casting vote of the chairman P.J. O'Neill.[51]

Seán Ó Luing, a biographer of both Arthur Griffith and Thomas Ashe, described Lawless as among the important members (*daoine tábhachtacha*) of Sinn Féin in 1908, alongside Thomas Clarke, Seán Mac Diarmada and Countess Markievicz, when Sinn Féin was discussing running candidates in local elections.[52] Thomas Bateman, Malahide, and R. Wogan, Garristown, successful candidates in the rural district council elections, agreed to sign the National Council pledge, broadly supporting Sinn Féin policies. The Swords branch put on lectures with eminent speakers such as James (Seamus) Deakin, a senior IRB organizer, inviting local United Irish League and labour union members to debate Sinn Féin policy. The message of self-reliance – Sinn Féin means 'ourselves alone' – was emphasized by its leader, Arthur Griffith, 'to make England take one hand from Ireland's throat and the other out of Ireland's pocket'.[53] By 1909, Lawless would welcome a new enthusiast to the Fingal Gaelic League, who would collaborate with him in a number of organizations: Thomas Ashe. Sinn Féin presented an intellectual alternative to those disaffected or disillusioned by the tight and the seemingly closed elite United Irish League-Irish Parliamentary Party consensus of large farmers.[54] Lawless would have been exposed to the energy and stimulation offered by Griffith and the other leading personalities in Sinn Féin at this time, developing politically from experiencing the matrix of nationalist organizations in which he was involved.[55]

The success of the wider Gaelic revival and Irish Ireland movements was in providing an outlet for the increased desire for an alternative identity, culture and philosophy. The branch meetings, classes, pageants and *feiseanna* of the Gaelic League, the games of the GAA, the confident debate of the Irish Ireland, National Council and Sinn Féin movements, and the romance of the literary revival together had an energizing, educating and empowering effect for a new generation of Irish people, educated, and with improving circumstances. They provided a healthy moral outlet for young people against the influence of English popular culture and the 'national curse of Ireland', excessive drinking, allowing the church to lend its support. An advert promoting the benefits of Irish classes with the Gaelic League in Skerries as a wholesome activity for children specifically targeted parents and the church. Many clerics were mindful of the opportunity for religious instruction afforded by the teaching of Irish and Christian history. Lusk Gaelic League, run by the local parish priest, included the rosary for children as an activity. Prominent in this branch was John Rooney, the son of Edward Rooney, a Dublin county councillor from 1899 to 1902. The building of libraries through the county, many funded by the Scottish-American philanthropist Andrew Carnegie, helped the growth of the Gaelic League, providing greater exposure to Irish literature, history and culture, despite some opposition to the holding of classes in public buildings. These informal educational and covert networking opportunities were embraced and utilized to optimum effect by the revolutionary underground, which was starting to reassert its presence, preparing for a day when their opportunity to strike might come again.

When P.J. O'Neill won back the Swords seat on the county council in 1908, he defeated P.J. Kettle. Kettle had had only put his name forward for the county council election, and Balrothery rural district council voted not to co-opt any members, denying Kettle a second chance. He transferred his energies to the Gaelic League, United Irish League and Farmers' Association. E.H. Woods was similarly excluded, but offered to continue to serve on hospital boards, if requested. A presentation made to Kettle by his supporters, at his home, in recognition of his nine years of public service, appeared to signal the end of his political career. While those who had been close to him, like Lawless, were present, there were no notable members of the Kettle family mentioned.[56] Among some of the larger landowners there seemed to be no political successors. The earl of Howth, related by marriage to both the Domville and Guinness families, died in 1909, and Sir Roger Palmer died in May 1910, without issue. The second Lord Holmpatrick, a military man, had little interest in politics.[57]

The following month, the House of Lords' rejection of Lloyd George's budget would trigger a constitutional crisis that would present a major opportunity for Redmond and the Irish Parliamentary Party.

3. On the brink: national and local politics converge, 1910–14

The January 1910 general election saw the balance of power revert to the Irish Parliamentary Party, and as a result, the prospect of home rule arose again. Sitting MP J.J. Clancy was returned unopposed. United Irish League meetings were the best attended in a number of years; Thomas McMahon, Michael Dunne, P.J. Kettle and Andrew Mooney were all prominent in their continued support of John Redmond.[1]

Ties of marriage and family further strengthened nationalist alliances. District councillor Nicholas Long of Swords, treasurer of the local United Irish League and committee member of the County Dublin Farmers' Association, was a brother-in-law of Edward McMahon, poor law guardian, of Gaybrook, Malahide, who died in 1910. McMahon's eldest daughter, Nan, would marry Thomas Smyth, magistrate and district councillor, in 1914. McMahon's son, also named Edward, would be elected a councillor. Edward had been in the same year in Blackrock College in 1901 as Edward Rooney, of Raheny, Lusk, prominent in the Gaelic League and later in the Irish Volunteers.[2] In 1894, Julia Lawless, Frank's sister, married Richard J. Rooney of Wyanstown House, Oldtown, chairman of the Balrothery rural district council, and a Dublin county councillor from 1902 to 1905.[3] When P.J. Kettle succeeded Frank Lawless as president of the Swords Gaelic League, Lawless remained treasurer, and his wife and daughter were elected to the committee. Col. Richard Woods replaced his brother E.H. Woods on the finance committee of the Balrothery poor law board of guardians. Attendance at meetings of the board of guardians declined, the traditional attendees, such as Col. Forster of Swords, being the notable exceptions. Due to the low attendance, many meetings were cancelled. The reduced status of the guardians' responsibilities in local government undoubtedly carried less interest for nationalist members.[4]

P.J. O'Neill became chairman of the general council of county councils, as local councillors pressed for a fairer taxation burden for Ireland and voiced concerns over the administration of the Pensions Act. He was also involved in the temperance movement, a key speaker at the Total Abstinence Congress held in Sackville Street in Dublin in June 1914, which an estimated 50,000 people attended. He outlined the 'influence of temperance in achieving Ireland's freedom', citing the poverty, hardship and sorrow that abuse of drink caused in Irish life. Ancient Order of Hibernians (AOH) branches were set up across the Fingal area from 1912, primarily to operate as benevolent societies for pension administration.[5]

Differences between nationalist representatives now started to manifest themselves in the council rooms, after years of polite consensus. Frank Lawless, now a declared Sinn Féin candidate, failed to secure a seat on Balrothery rural district council in the 1911 local elections, defeated by a margin of eight votes in Swords West, the same ward in which P.J. Kettle had been elected to Dublin county council in 1902. The first council meeting in June proved a stormy affair, with the practice of co-option being defeated on a vote of 17 to 13, and R.J. Rooney being challenged for the chair but holding on against Michael Dunne, again by 17 to 13. A.S. Hussey retained the vice chair unanimously, but the debate indicated that it may have been a gesture to a token unionist, albeit a Catholic and an experienced and able public servant. The same sentiments surfaced the following year at the annual re-election of Captain Vesey of Lucan as vice chairman of Dublin county council. Nationalist rivalries continued later in that month, when a co-option to Balrothery rural district council was required for the Kilsallaghan seat. Rooney proposed his brother-in-law Frank Lawless, but P.J. Kettle, his close neighbour and long-time colleague, won the vote 15 to 3. Rooney accused an 'All for Swords League' clique of combining against Lawless, and Kettle expressed his personal regret that Lawless had opposed him.[6] Lawless would face further opposition later in the year when Fr Mulcahy, parish priest of Swords and chairman of the local library committee, objected to a Gaelic League fundraising event at the library. The row ended up on the council where the Chairman Rooney and Fr Mulcahy disagreed strongly, the proceedings all duly reported in the press.[7]

According to police reports, 1910 was peaceful in Fingal, with little political activity and a good harvest, the usual branches of nationalist sentiment meeting irregularly. RIC County Inspector Reginald Heard reported in October that 'county Dublin was peaceful' and 'the farmers of county Dublin are all well-to-do men and the harvest has been a good one'. Agrarian tensions surfaced in 1911 in Garristown in relation to the redistribution of local estates by the estates commissioners, amid fears of outside graziers securing land ahead of local tenants. The impending sales of the Rooney estate of approximately 300 acres and the Digby estate of approximately 200 acres heightened local tensions, particularly when a Mr P.K. Joyce of Westport secured an interim lease there and stocked the estate with his bullock herd. Joyce was put under police watch as the United Irish League threatened cattle drives, and MP Clancy raised the matter in parliament. Local United Irish League councillor Andrew Mooney got involved in the demonstrations, and the priority of the motions at the local meetings is informative, demonstrating the United Irish League and Irish Parliamentary Party attempts to control the agenda of any mass activity. Motions passed first called for home rule and support for Redmond, before condemning police activity and calling for untenanted lands for local tenants. In February 1912, Clancy called on the local United Irish League to desist from objecting to grazier leases until the sale process was complete. By the end of 1912, when the Digby estate at Oldtown was sold, the police reported that the locals were pleased with the outcome. Agitators targeted part of the Aungier estates near Swords in late 1911, about 200 acres belonging to Mary Aungier. A number of graves were dug in a field, with farm manager A. Plunkett identified, and a temporary headstone bearing the message 'these graves are for the land grabbers of this estate'. Local United Irish League officers and Clancy condemned these outrages, although at the same time they encouraged land redistribution, seeking to control its progression. The Aungier estate was eventually offered for private sale.[8]

The mainstream nationalist movement continued to enjoy clerical support, with Fr McDonnell elected vice president of St Margaret's United Irish League alongside P.J. Kettle, under the leadership of Michael Dunne, reflecting what Lyons called its 'dominant position in the life of the country up to 1914'.[9] When Douglas Hyde and The O'Rahilly attended a Gaelic League function at Lusk, James Stack, clerk of Balrothery rural district council and former clerk of the board of guardians, read the address in Irish. The president of Lusk branch was local parish priest Fr O'Byrne.[10] Arthur Griffith and William O'Brien remained critical of Redmond's ability to deliver effective home rule, or were suspicious of whether Asquith would grant it, and continued to highlight the failure to secure any other meaningful concessions ahead of home rule.[11] The singular quest for home rule had long led to the rejection of various interim measures. The rejection of the 1907 council bill, a step closer to home rule that might have maintained a united Ireland within the United Kingdom or the empire while devolving further local power to Ireland, appears in hindsight to have been a short-sighted and self-serving move by the leaders of constitutional nationalism. The failure or inability of Redmond and Dillon to acknowledge or accept the potential of the bill, the drafting of which they had influenced, as a step on the road to home rule, or adequately or realistically address the concerns of unionists, is central to the thesis of the missed opportunity.[12] It is ironic that after years of struggle, Michael Collins would later coin a phrase, highly applicable here, when he said that the Anglo-Irish Treaty gave 'the freedom to achieve freedom'.[13] One can but speculate on how effective a series of gradual steps might have been at this earlier stage. The accommodation of unionist and nationalist that was facilitated by working together for common benefit at local council level saw unionists Col. Woods and Anthony Hussey attend the unveiling of the Parnell monument in October 1911, jointly representing Balrothery rural district council and poor law guardians. When there was an outbreak of foot-and-mouth disease in Fingal in the summer of 1912, the earl of Fingall and Sir Horace Plunkett, who were related, met with P.J. O'Neill, Richard J. Rooney, Thomas Aungier and MP William Field to press for government intervention and aid. Dublin county council strongly protested against the closure of Dublin port, which was seen as an opportunistic effort to aid English livestock farmers. The boundary between those who favoured union and those who saw Ireland's position as self-governing within the empire did not appear so wide. However, in the unionist-controlled townships, there was resistance to increasingly nationalist motions. For example, Kingstown urban district council strongly rejected a Dublin county council objection to the appointment of an Englishman, Mr Arthur Norway, as head of the post office in Ireland.[14]

J.J. Lee maintains that the new local political elite 'became as corrupt as the old one', with favouritism commonplace. He attributes a lack of candidates of vision or ability graduating to national politics to such a system of appointments.[15] This, however, misses the point that there was no formal party political structure, with the United Irish League a support organization rather than closely integrated with the Irish Parliamentary Party. Local representatives were primarily representing their local community and their own family, class or regional interests first, whether for personal gain or civic responsibility. They were no more self-serving than the senior members of the Irish Parliamentary Party, and were just as ambitious for advancement.[16] In 1913, local district councillors R.J. Rooney, Archdale Graham, chairman of Balbriggan town commissioners, and Thomas Smyth were appointed magistrates. In May 1914, the council appointed Rooney as poor-rate collector for Dublin, but he had to delay taking up the post until his membership of the county committee of the department of agriculture and technical instruction expired.[17] Laurence O'Neill, son of Joseph O'Neill, chairman of North Dublin rural district council, was solicitor to Balrothery rural district council, and electoral returning officer for Dublin county council. Christopher Friery, born in Swords, who worked as J.J. Clancy's election agent, was also coroner for north Co. Dublin. By the end of 1914, P.J. Kettle and Michael Dunne had joined the O'Neill cousins on the magistrates' bench.[18] Coincidentally, Joseph O'Neill's sons Gerald and Kevin played cricket for Malahide on the same team as Tom Kettle in 1910.[19] Tom Kettle, son of Andrew, was a cousin of P.J. Kettle, but after his initial involvement in the North Dublin United Irish League, he did not continue in local politics, instead serving as an MP for East Tyrone and becoming professor of economics at University College Dublin. He and his close friend Francis Skeffington were both married to daughters of the MP David Sheehy, Francis to Hannah, and Tom Kettle to Mary.[20]

When the home rule bill passed its third reading in the House of Commons in January 1913, a series of motions congratulating Redmond and the Irish Parliamentary Party followed at the local level, with some unionist dissent in Balrothery rural district council from Hussey and Woods. Captain Vesey, on Dublin county council, emphasized that from a financial viewpoint it was a very bad bill for Ireland.[21] Police reports indicated that matters were peaceful and, noting the number of organizations in existence, doubted their activity. There were at this time 12 branches of the United Irish League, 13 of the Ancient Order of Hibernians, 6 of the Gaelic League, 6 of the National Foresters, 6 of the Land and Labour League, 3 of Fianna Éireann boy scouts, 2 of the Town

9. County Dublin Farmers' Association, 1907 (courtesy of Swords Historical Society)

Tenants League and one of Sinn Féin. Police intelligence reports tended to lump them all in together as broadly disloyal.[22]

Farming in the Fingal area in 1913 was characterised by grazing and cattle fattening in the north and west of the county with a concentration on more labour-intensive tillage farming in the southern and eastern parts. Crops such as corn, oats and barley for the brewing and distilling industries in Dublin city grew alongside fruit, vegetables and potatoes for the Dublin markets. In addition to large ascendancy estates,[23] there was a growing number of sizeable holdings built up by Catholic nationalist farmers, who had benefitted from the reforms following the land agitation of the 1880s, and the subsequent land purchase acts. These farmers constituted a new progressive elite, an economic and political class, who, in addition to introducing new farming methods, were at the heart of local politics, occupying influential positions as poor law guardians and as local county and district councillors.

During 1913, city-based organizers of Larkin's Irish Transport and General Workers' Union began recruiting members in the Fingal area on farms that directly supplied the Dublin markets, identifying and harnessing issues of discontent among the farm-labouring class. They began by recruiting members among those conveying farm produce to the Dublin markets, and then recruited in the towns and villages of Fingal, where many of the farm labourers lived in lodging houses. The result was a strike for better pay and conditions in late July, which targeted the imminent harvest on those farms owned by the nationalist political elite, in a year in which a bumper crop was expected. The County Dublin Farmers' Association met in August and came to a negotiated agreement with the strikers, in order to protect their livelihood – the harvest. However, within a fortnight events in the city on Bloody Sunday, 31 August 1913, would escalate matters, turning the strike into a lockout and an industrial dispute into a political one over union membership and the threat of socialism, which would drag on for the next six months.[24] William Martin Murphy called on his fellow employers in the farming community and his nationalist United Irish League colleagues not to employ transport union labour, and they responded. The farming elite in Fingal met the threat to their wealth and status from this convergence of class, agrarian and political issues head on, led by the Kettle and O'Neill families, with nationalist and unionist landowners and farmers standing together.

A close examination of who was involved, their motivations, convictions and responses reveals the deeper underlying issues that drove the intensity on both sides. This was not just a dispute with the Protestant unionist landlords of old but primarily with Catholic nationalist employers. This was not about tenant and landlord, but labourer and farmer. These were the farmers and families, most of whom, a generation earlier, had been involved in the struggles of the Land League to secure rights for tenants, but they were now on the other side. This agrarian conflict in Fingal was a precursor of the fractures in nationalism that would occur in 1914 at the outbreak of the First World War, as well as in 1916, in 1918, and in 1922 and its aftermath. Socialism, Larkinism, trade unionism and republican nationalism were now emerging to compete with constitutional nationalism and unionism in a revolutionary period that would culminate in both self-determination and a civil war. The class conflict of the Lockout of 1913 would merge with the nationalist conflict, consistent with the United Irish League and Irish Parliamentary Party attempts at control over the previous 20 years, but not with the results they imagined.

The farm proprietors of north Dublin in 1913 were organized and experienced, determined to protect the prosperity they had gained on the back of political struggle and land purchase, and were capable of taking on the Irish Transport and General Workers' Union (ITGWU). Their relative activities up to and during the Lockout, highlight not alone growing class division and discontent, but a struggle to control and influence agricultural labour. Previous landlord wealth may have been generated from land ownership alone, but the wealth of the farmer was derived from the produce of that land, and for the tillage farmers of north Dublin the harvest was critical. Crucial to that harvest was labour. It is, therefore, unsurprising that the harvest was at the core of the conflict, as it was at the heart of the farming cycle.

Andrew Kettle coordinated the importation of 'free labour' to save the harvest, bypassing union labour, under police protection. In some cases, in the absence of available labour, the larger farmers themselves saved the harvest, such as when several justices of the peace and gentleman farmers harvested 16 acres of corn at the farm at Kilmore, Artane, of Charles Kettle, son of Andrew Kettle and brother of former MP Thomas Kettle. The 20 or so gentlemen were collected and conveyed by motor car by the magistrate Mr Dodd of Cloghran.[25] P.J. Kettle, at his farm at The Leas, Swords, had help from neighbouring farmers to bring in his harvest, as well as from a number of his men who had returned to work at the start of October.[26] The *Drogheda Independent* of 20 September 1913 reported that 30 union men had stacked corn at the farm of Frank Lawless' brother Edward (Ned) at Balheary, Swords, because he was 'not a member of the County Dublin Farmers' Association, did not object to the ITGWU, and was relatively poor'.

Joseph O'Neill instigated the eviction of strikers from labourers' cottages on his land, implemented by the landowner magistracy at the petty sessions.[27] A number of farmers from Kinsealy, Swords and Ballymun applied at the Swords petty sessions for repossession of cottages from striking labourers. Labourers would now face eviction from farmers who had fought against landlord evictions a generation earlier. Some of the magistrates – Col. Hely-Hutchinson, Col. Forster, John Cuffe and Joseph Christie – were themselves landowners and farmers in the area. Defending counsel objected, but the magistrates still heard the cases.[28] Christie had been a committee member of the County Dublin Farmers' Association going back many years.[29] Cuffe was a district councillor, and involved with the County Dublin Farmers' Association. The cases involved incidents of boycotting and intimidation against both farmers and workers and their families, and the turning loose of horses and sheep.[30]

Matters escalated with rioting at Swords in October continuing over a number of nights, and a number of suspicious burnings, after which the arrests of union leaders and agitators effectively crushed the strikers, who were facing into a cold and hungry winter.[31] Incidents of intimidation of 'scabs' and alleged strike-breakers had increased in Swords, mainly in relation to the serving of drink in pubs, and this culminated in full-blown riots over a couple of nights, 8 and 9 October. Following a meeting in the town at a house nicknamed 'Liberty Hall', the strikers attempted to stop a large drove of cattle and sheep passing through to Dublin from a farm in Gormanstown. The animals were stopped, and then driven back through the town. Police responded by baton-charging the strikers, and rioting followed, with a number of arrests made, and considerable damage to properties on Main Street.[32] There were sporadic incidents on the second night, including attempts to damage properties in Kinsealy. Further arrests were made in later days, followed by convictions for rioting and intimidation.[33] When union organizer Frank Moss was imprisoned in Mountjoy Gaol on 24 October, he immediately began a hunger strike, and was initially forcibly fed. He continued on hunger strike intermittently through most of his three-month sentence.[34]

10. Main Street, Swords, Co. Dublin, where riots occurred on 8 Oct. 1913.

With the formation of the Ulster Volunteer Force in January 1913, Ulster unionists increased their fundraising, recruiting and drilling, to resist any implementation of home rule. The Irish Parliamentary Party leadership continued to dismiss this opposition as a bluff from Edward Carson.[35] It was almost the end of the year before the Irish National Volunteers formed under the leadership of Eoin MacNeill in November 1913. Andrew Kettle's sons, Laurence and Tom Kettle, were to play prominent roles; both were on the committee, with Laurence as secretary, although Tom was not well enough to attend the inaugural meeting at the Rotunda, in Dublin.[36]

Thomas Ashe went to the United States in January 1914 with Diarmuid Lynch to raise money for the Gaelic League, returning to Ireland on the outbreak of the war, while Lynch remained, engaged in IRB duties with Clan na Gael.[37] Ashe was a frequent visitor to the Coleman house in Swords, and, like Lynch, was a Gaelic League officer. Popular locally, with striking looks, Ashe was a good singer and sportsman. He did not get on with Fr Byrne, president of Lusk Gaelic League, who was a supporter of the Irish Parliamentary Party and member of the United Irish League.[38]

In March 1914, James Connolly spoke in Swords to raise an Irish Citizen Army (ICA) company, at a meeting attended by Countess Markievicz, Jim Larkin and Captain Jack White, which five hundred people attended, including the recently released local union leader Frank Moss, who was a member of the army executive committee of the Citizen Army.[39] Some 80 members enlisted, and Frank Carroll, Dublin Street, Swords, was appointed secretary.

In June, police reported the defections of Citizen Army members to the Irish Volunteers, and noted the involvement of Tom Kettle, R.J. Rooney, James Lawless, Balrothery union medical officer Dr May, and William Bannon, the Balbriggan town clerk. Thomas McDonagh spoke at a meeting in Swords, starting a Volunteer company in April 1914 with cousins William and Richard Coleman in joint command of over 50 recruits.[40] Irish Volunteer companies were set up across Fingal in the early months of 1914 – at Skerries, Balbriggan and Lusk in May. Following the Curragh incident in March, and the landing of arms at Larne by the Ulster Volunteer Force (UVF) in April, Dublin unionists meeting at the Shelbourne Hotel in April 1914 feared a looming civil war, 'brought about by *this* government's persistence in introducing Home Rule'.[41]

Newspapers reported the results of the 1914 local elections as a defeat for socialism, Michael Dunne claiming a victory for 'Faith and Fatherland', the cry of the nationalist party. Larkinite candidates were defeated in both council and district elections, but Frank Lawless was successful for Sinn Féin, finally topping the poll in Swords West. A 'progressive' evangelist, Benjamin Newcombe, from Howth, defeated Joseph O'Neill, chairman of North Dublin RDC. Ms Molly Adrian, later active in the rebellion as a member of Cumann na mBan, was elected as the first woman guardian in Balrothery in 1914, and was cheered on her entry to the meeting room for the first time.[42] Michael Dunne, together with Laurence Kettle, were prominently involved, according to local police intelligence, in the landing of arms at Howth in July 1914, and their distribution in the Fingal area. Police estimated that the bulk of rifles in the north county ended up in Skerries.[43]

An indication of the depth of antagonism to Sinn Féin among some nationalists manifested itself in the reaction to a request to Balrothery poor law guardians in April 1914 for support for a Sinn Féin resolution opposing partition in the event of home rule. Amid laughter, chairman Hartford suggested that such a resolution was only fit for burning, and instructed the clerk to throw it in the fire. The episode highlights the extent of the naivety and smugness of some nationalists regarding the threat of partition and the resolve of Ulster unionists to oppose home rule.[44] Redmond's insistence on appointing his nominees to the executive of the Volunteers was a further example of the Irish Parliamentary Party's tendency to attempt to control any potential nationalist mass movement in Ireland. This was now more pertinent, as home rule was imminent and there was a fear of anything that might compromise or impede its introduction, as police reports had indicated for some time.[45] Maume explains that Redmond 'saw himself as leader of the nation with a national cause, rather than as party leader'.[46] His supporters at the national and local levels likewise saw themselves as part of a government in waiting, as Pašeta has argued, not to be denied by either unionist or extreme nationalists.[47] Tensions in Ireland were escalating, with guns landed by the Irish Volunteers at Howth on 26 July, and the emotional public funerals of those killed at Bachelors Walk in Dublin in the aftermath. The addition of guns in two private armies added a new and explosive dimension to the increasingly sectarian political scene. Civil war in Ireland loomed just as war in Europe seemed inevitable.

Local politicians took opposing positions on the unfolding international events. Dunne, the Balrothery rural district council's chairman, at a review of the St Margaret's Volunteers corps with Laurence Kettle, pledged their support to defend home rule and place themselves at Redmond's command. Dunne's speech, reported in the *Drogheda Independent* on 7 September 1914, is indicative of the self-congratulatory rhetoric and the general excitement caused by the placing of home rule of the statute book, and of the outbreak of the war:

> We desire to make it perfectly clear that the Volunteer corps in our district will act in perfect harmony with Mr Redmond and the Irish Party, towards whom we entertain feelings of the warmest admiration and confidence, and to whom we pledge our solid and hearty support, in whatever course they may decide to be best for preserving to our people the secure enjoyment of the long laboured-for and yearningly desired blessings of self-government.[48]

J.P. Cuffe warned at a Balrothery board of guardians meeting that:

> if England becoming embroiled in the impending international conflict looked to Ireland for recruits, the answer from the nationalists would be that she had better take care of her own troubles, or at all events, confine her recruiting activities to the favoured North-East corner.[49]

Local differences on the issue of the war surfaced months before Redmond's speech at Woodenbridge on 20 September 1914, generally given as the occasion of the subsequent Volunteer split. Police reports in the summer of 1914 noted the militancy of the Swords Volunteers. The local AOH and clergy did not support them, and the membership was 'mostly farmers' sons, labourers and shop assistants' with 'nobody of influence' involved. Swords company split in August, with the majority Redmondite, but significantly, the officers recorded as siding with 'Sinn Féin'. This label was used loosely by police to describe militant nationalists, but did not mean they were members. An estimate of the strength of the Swords breakaway in September was 44, 22 of whom had arms. Further splits followed Redmond's Woodenbridge call to arms.[50] Lusk company had already split because of a row between rival families over who should be in command, and half their number left.[51] By December 1914, RIC Intelligence estimated that the 260 Irish Volunteers in the whole of Co. Dublin had only 78 rifles between them.[52]

The potentially explosive sequence of events from 1912, born of Ulster opposition to home rule, and continuing through to the outbreak of war in

August 1914, brought about greater politicization in local councils, and further divided the local political elite. The outbreak of war may have averted civil war in Ireland, but the divisions on the island would remain unreconciled.

A review of the nominal roll of Irish Volunteer officers from Fingal who mustered and fought in 1916 contains individuals who were active within the cultural movement but also sons of active nationalist councillors and prominent United Irish League members.[53] Thomas Ashe, a schoolteacher, originally from Co. Kerry, was in command at Ashbourne, with Dr Richard Hayes, Balrothery union medical officer, as his adjutant and intelligence officer. Captain Edward (Ned) Rooney of Lusk was a prominent member of both the GAA and the Gaelic League. He had attended Blackrock College, where Eamon de Valera taught, and was the son of Edward Rooney, the former Dublin county councillor from 1899 to 1902. His brother John was a rural district councillor in Balrothery, and their younger brother James also fought.[54] The Rooney brothers were renowned pipers and played alongside Ashe with the Fingal Ravens Pipe Band. Captain Richard Coleman of Swords came from a family active in the Gaelic League, and was son of the local schoolmaster and sacristan at St Colmcille's Church, Swords. He had been jointly the first commanding officer of the Swords company of Irish Volunteers, with his cousin William Coleman. William enlisted with the Royal Irish Regiment after the split, and was killed in France in 1917, with the rank of sergeant, commanding a trench mortar battery.[55] Frank Lawless, the veteran political influence on separatist nationalism in Fingal, was battalion quartermaster, and his sons Lieutenant Joseph and Colm would fight, along with his brothers Edward (Ned) and James, a captain with the St Margaret's company, and assistant secretary of Dublin county council. His sister Mary and daughters Kathleen and Eibhlin took part as members of Cumann na nBan. Colm Lawless later became a student at St Enda's College, Rathfarnham.[56] The Crennigan brothers and James Marks, employees of Frank Lawless, and a couple of ex-pupils of Thomas Ashe, the Kelly brothers, would be among the 70 combatants. Lieutenant Charles Weston of Turvey, Donabate, was the remaining local officer, also a member of the Black Raven Pipe Band, started in Lusk in 1910 by Ashe and John Rooney, DC.[57] Bernard McAllister, Swords company, also of Turvey, was son of district councillor Christopher McAllister, himself a Redmondite Volunteer, and would marry Kathleen Lawless in 1929. On hearing of the split in the Swords Volunteers, the younger McAllister rushed to his father's house and removed the guns stored there, lest they be used by the 'other side'.[58] Five members of the Lusk team that won the Dublin junior hurling championship in 1915 would fight. Forty-two of those who would muster in Easter Week were members of local GAA clubs.[59] Joseph Lawless relates in his Bureau of Military History witness statement that his uncle, Edward Lawless, had travelled to South Africa in 1902 to fight with the Boers, but arrived in the Transvaal as hostilities ceased, and also recounts his father's IRB activities, especially in the infiltration of other organizations.

Several accounts show Frank Lawless prominent in IRB circles in Dublin. A troop or '*sluagh*' of Fianna Éireann boy scouts formed at Swords in 1911, with the Lawless farm used for the boys' camps.[60] F.X. Martin refers to Lawless at a general council meeting of the Irish National Volunteers on 6 December 1914 as the Co. Dublin representative, and Ó Snodaigh includes him as an IRB member in attendance at the Volunteer conference in October 1915, in addition to those 14 members on the executive.[61]

Conclusion

The period 1891 to 1914 is one of local political evolution, and the changing elites in Fingal reflect the progress of this evolution. If the land acts began the transfer of influence from the unionist landowning elite, then the Local Government Act completed the job by transferring local political influence to the nationalist farmer and merchant elite, and introduced a new independent-minded activist to the local elite. It signalled the start of a move from affluence-endowed to representative influence, when influencers became leaders. Comerford's analysis of nationalism, referencing Anderson's 'imagined communities' concept, provides a useful approach to understanding the changing interactions and motivations of the political elites of Fingal.[1] The differences that caused so much turmoil in the first decades of the 20th century, and beyond, relate essentially to the relationship of Ireland with Britain, whether Ireland's future lay within the union, within the empire or as a completely separate entity. These political convictions were a reflection of the three different identities, a combination of religious, social, political and cultural identity, found in Fingal at this time, each with a different 'imagined nation' in mind for Ireland. But until partition became reality, it was different imaginations of the same nation. The civic duty and the genuinely held convictions of unionists like Colonel Forster and A.S. Hussey confirm this.

For the elites of Fingal, the political and social aspects of life were inseparable. The class of local power brokers that dominated between the decline of the landed ascendancy class and the coming of the post-revolutionary elite were the Catholic strong farmers who benefitted from the Land War and were the standard-bearers for home rule, and their political leadership, the Irish Parliamentary Party. The boundaries between the different political and social elites are notable in the potential for merging and crossover, which occurred from unionist to nationalist and from nationalist to republican. The Irish Catholic landlord subculture identified by Leeann Lane, which had connected to the ruling class above through social status and to the lower class below through religion,[2] moved closer in economic and social respects to what remained of the constitutional nationalist elite. They eventually became politically homogeneous in the new state.

Emmet Larkin identified an Irish nation with an increasingly central Catholicism providing a substitute for the lost Gaelic culture and declining Irish language after the Famine, such that by 1914 'Irish' and 'Catholic' were interchangeable.[3] This *Irish state* 'was created in the minds of Irishmen'[4] when in 1886, the Land League, Fenians and Irish Parliamentary Party came to an accommodation with the Catholic church, forming a constitutional consensus with one leader, one party machine, press control and a single-plank programme: home rule. The threat that this posed to the old ascendancy elite, accompanied by the marginalization of the Catholic lower middle class, provides the background narrative for the changes in Fingal politics. The longer this goal took to realise, the greater the potential for its enemies on both sides to organize against it. Hutchinson identified the development of cultural nationalism, providing an alternative identity, which would challenge home rule, from its linguistic Gaelic origins to an articulation of Irish identity that would result in the revolutionary movement that secured independence.[5] This third emerging elite appealed to the young educated Catholics, who coveted opportunity, but who experienced 'blocked mobility' from both the Protestant and Catholic dominating elites, and between generations.[6]

The broader Irish Ireland and Gaelic revival showed that there was 'more to nationhood than a particular constitutional status'.[7] The movement was not as narrow as some history has written it, on the evidence of its branch activities and participants found in this study. Identity provided an alternative to material influence, allowing an intellectual self-confidence to develop. The writings of Griffith, Hyde, Moran, Yeats and Pearse all made different contributions to the emergent identity of a self-reliant, de-anglicized Irish Ireland, constructing a past in their own image of a future that would ultimately drive the independence struggle. The Irish Agricultural Organisation Society, set up in 1894 by unionist MP Sir Horace Plunkett, made its contribution to independent commercial thinking.[8] The educational, communal and local nature of cultural nationalism gave it an egalitarian dimension, in contrast to the centralized controls of national and local political nationalism. There was a receptive audience, if not for change then for the opportunity to express one's own unique identity.[9] This new influence of intellect and emotion was starting to displace the traditional influence of wealth.

Hutchinson's description of the Irish Parliamentary Party as 'an ageing oligarchy, preoccupied with parliamentary manoeuvre' is central to their eventual rejection, and applicable in Fingal to the local nationalist and unionist elites. Both held on to power to an extent that the next generation either was unable to inherit, was uninterested or had moved beyond to a revolutionary position.[10] Tom Kettle and his cohorts epitomize this. Suspicious of the Gaelic revivalists, but more liberal and progressive than their parents' generation, this group felt their ascent to leadership was blocked by a generation unwilling to give up the power and influence that they themselves had assumed since the 1880s.[11]

Comerford reminds us that the great constant of history is the 'manoeuvring for survival and advancement of self and family through access to material resources and socio-political advantage'.[12] This constant is evident in the changing elites in Fingal in the period under review, each group striving for its own ascendancy relative to the others. In 1909, a police report on the

United Irish League in Swords concluded that 'members do not appear to join with any intention of pressing any important Irish question, but to use it as a lever for personal benefit for themselves should the opportunity arise'.[13] The realities of local politics and the acceptance of a changing world are reflected in the pragmatic approaches of Thomas Aungier and T.W. Hamlet at election time. P.J. Kettle embraced the potential of the cultural revival but remained true to his constitutional principles despite rejection. That there was not a greater accommodation nationally between moderate unionism and moderate nationalism, when evidence suggests that they could work together for common objectives at local council level, must remain an indictment of those at the extremes of both traditions. Despite progress and improvements, there were missed opportunities, arising from generations of mutual mistrust, of personal convictions and aspirations, but also of simple self-interest. The rejection of the 1907 Irish council bill by all sides underscores this. Travers fittingly described the period from 1870 to 1922 as one of 'settlements, attempted settlements, and divisions'.[14]

The movement and interaction of the elites in north Dublin must be viewed in the context of the wider ongoing settlement of the land question and its effect on national and local politics. The changing ownership demographic manifested itself in Fingal through changing degrees of involvement in local politics. The volume of evidence consulted for this book indicates that there is considerable further opportunity to research this changing demographic.

The alternative and parallel evolution was the realization that perceived progress was limited and that the establishment would never yield willingly or fully to demands for Irish self-determination. This view of advanced – if not physical-force – nationalists saw the Irish Parliamentary Party and John Redmond as an intrinsic part of that establishment. In Fingal, the strong farmer and merchant class, the main beneficiaries of the land purchase programme and influential incumbents in the key positions of local government, were the disciples and foundations of that same establishment, and were becoming more so by 1914. The story of Frank Lawless of Swords, his political education and migration to revolutionary politics epitomizes this disillusionment. Lawless died in an accident in 1922, aged 52 years, never having fulfilled his political destiny. The attendance at his funeral, which included Michael Collins, Arthur Griffith, Eamon de Valera and detachments of all five battalions of the Dublin Brigade, is testimony to the respect in which he was held as a senior republican.[15]

The rebellion of 1916 and its aftermath enabled the advanced nationalist elite effectively to leapfrog the government-in-waiting of constitutional nationalism, which never attained full power. Lyons described the eventual preservation of continuity between 'the (IPP) party that had experience and no power and the Dáil that had power and no experience'.[16] How that continuity played itself out in the next era of local politics and changing elites in Fingal is a story that remains to be written.

Notes

ABBREVIATIONS

AOH	Ancient Order of Hibernians
BMH WS	Bureau of Military History' Witness Statement
CO	Colonial Office
DC	district councillor
DL	deputy lieutenant
FCCA	Fingal County Council Archives
GAA	Gaelic Athletic Association
HC	House of Commons
ICA	Irish Citizen Army
IRB	Irish Republican Brotherhood
ITGWU	Irish Transport and General Workers' Union
JP	justice of the peace
MA	Military Archives
MP	member of parliament
MS	manuscript
NUI	National University of Ireland
PLG	poor law guardian
PLU	poor law union
RDC	rural district council
RIC	Royal Irish Constabulary
UCD	University College Dublin
UIL	United Irish League
UVF	Ulster Volunteer Force

INTRODUCTION

1 F.S.L. Lyons, 'The aftermath of Parnell, 1891–1903' and 'The watershed, 1903–7' in W.E. Vaughan (ed.), *A new history of Ireland*, vi: *Ireland under the union II, 1870–1921* (Oxford, 1996), pp 81–122.

2 J.J. Lee, *The modernisation of Irish society, 1848–1918* (Dublin, 1973); D. George Boyce, *Nationalism in Ireland* (London, 1982), *Nineteenth-century Ireland: the search for stability* (Dublin, 1990) and *Ireland, 1828–1923: from ascendancy to democracy* (Oxford, 1992); Pauric Travers, *Settlements and divisions: Ireland, 1870–1922* (Dublin 1988); David Fitzpatrick, *The two Irelands, 1912–39* (Oxford, 1998); R.V. Comerford, *Ireland* (London, 2003); D. George Boyce and Alan O'Day (eds), *Ireland in transition, 1867–1921* (London, 2004).

3 Named after the leaders of the different factions, John Dillon, Joseph Devlin and John Redmond.

4 Padraig G. Lane, 'Agricultural labourers and rural violence, 1850–1914', *Studia Hibernica*, 27 (1993), 77–87; *idem*, 'Agricultural labourers and the land question' in Carla King (ed.), *Famine, land and culture in Ireland* (Dublin, 2000), pp 101–15.

5 See also Terence Dooley, 'Landlords and the land question, 1879–1909' in King (ed.), *Famine, land and culture in Ireland*, pp 116–39.

6 Lawrence McBride, *The greening of Dublin castle: the transformation of bureaucratic and judicial personnel in Ireland, 1892–1922* (Washington, 1991); R.B. McDowell, *The Irish administration, 1801–1914* (Dublin, 1964).

7 Tom Garvin, *Nationalist revolutionaries in Ireland, 1858–1928* (Oxford, 1987) and *The evolution of Irish nationalist politics* (Dublin, 1981); John Hutchinson, *The dynamics of cultural nationalism: the Gaelic revival and the creation of the Irish nation state* (London, 1987).
8 BMH Witness Statements, Military Archives, Dublin, WS1043 Joseph V. Lawless, pp 1–11.
9 Michael Wheatley, *Nationalism and the Irish party: provincial Ireland, 1910–16* (Oxford, 2005); Fergus Campbell, *Land and revolution: nationalist politics in the west of Ireland, 1891–1921* (Oxford, 2005); Donnacha Sean Lucey, 'Land and popular politics in County Kerry, 1872–86' (PhD, NUI Maynooth, 2007).

1. FIN DE SIÈCLE, 1891–8

1 Christopher Ryan, *Lewis' Dublin – a topographical dictionary of the parishes, towns and villages of Dublin city and county* (Cork, 2001), pp 49–50.
2 Patrick Archer, *Fair Fingal* (2nd ed. Dublin, 1975), p. 1.
3 *Census of Ireland, 1891*, HC 1890–1 [C. 6515] xcv, 1.
4 *Agricultural statistics of Ireland, 1891*, HC 1892 [C. 6777] lxxxviii, 285.
5 Alexander Thom, *Thom's almanac and official directory of the United Kingdom and Ireland, 1891*, p. 1528.
6 Virginia Crossman, *Local government in nineteenth century Ireland* (Belfast, 1996); *eadem*, *Politics, pauperism and power in nineteenth century Ireland* (Manchester, 2006), pp 36–7; *eadem*, 'Peculation and partiality – local government in nineteenth-century rural Ireland' in Roger Swift and Christine Kinealy (eds), *Politics and power in Victorian Ireland* (Dublin, 2006), pp 133–42.
7 W.E. Vaughan, *Landlords and tenants in mid-Victorian Ireland* (Oxford, 1994), p. 104.
8 Terence Dooley, *The decline of the big house in Ireland: a study of Irish landed families, 1860–1960* (Dublin, 2001), p. 28.
9 Michael Davitt, *The fall of feudalism in Ireland or the story of the land league revolution* (London, 1904).
10 Fergus Campbell, *The Irish establishment, 1870–1914* (Oxford, 2009), p. 20.
11 John Bateman, *The great landowners of Great Britain and Ireland, 1883* (4th ed., London, 1970). These evaluations are based on the British House of Commons *Return of owners of land of one acre and upwards in counties, cities and towns in Ireland*, HC 1876 [C. 1492] lxxx, 61, and updated to 1883 by Bateman, in consultation with the major landowners.
12 Sir Bernard Burke, *Genealogical and heraldic history of the landed gentry of Ireland* (London, 1912), p. 118.
13 Dillon Cosgrave, *North Dublin* (Dublin, 1909), p. 31; Brian M. Walker (ed.), *Parliamentary election results in Ireland, 1801–1922* (Dublin, 1978), pp 272–3.
14 *Freeman's Journal*, 29 June 1865 and 13 Feb. 1883.
15 L.J. Kettle (ed.), *The material for victory – being the memoirs of Andrew J. Kettle* (Dublin, 1958), p. 17.
16 Desmond McCabe, 'Clancy, John Joseph' in James McGuire and James Quinn (eds), *Dictionary of Irish biography* (Cambridge, 2009).
17 Walker, *Parliamentary election results*, pp 348–9. Note that population is different to census, as parliamentary division is different.
18 A largely ceremonial crown appointment, deputising for the lord lieutenant, the crown representative in Ireland.
19 *Irish Times*, 1 Apr. 1891, 3 Mar. 1892, 17 Mar. 1893 and 21 Dec. 1894.
20 *Thom's Directory*, 1891, pp 1074–9, 1892 pp 884–5; Cosgrave, *North Dublin*, p. 27; Burke, *Dictionary of the landed gentry*, p. 511; *Genealogical and heraldic history of the landed gentry*, p. 778; *Commission of the peace (Ireland) – returns for each county, city and borough of the names of persons holding commission of the peace*, HC 1893–4 (463) lxxiv, 201, p. 40; *Irish Times*, 27 Apr. 1886.
21 *Irish Times*, 7 Nov. 1890.
22 *Unionist convention for the provinces of Leinster, Munster & Connaught – report of proceedings, lists of committees, delegates, etc.* (Dublin, 1892).
23 *Irish Times*, 16 Nov. 1893; *Irish Times*, 24 June 1920; *Freeman's Journal*, 30 Nov. 1887; *Commission of the peace (Ireland)*, HC 1893–4 (463) lxxiv, 201, p. 40; *Irish*

Times, 24 Mar. 1893; http://census.nationalarchives.ie/pages/1901/Dublin/Dalkey/Coliemore_Road/1316991.

24 Bateman, *Landowners*; minute book of Co. Dublin grand jury 1893, FCCA.

25 Minute book of Co. Dublin grand jury 1893, FCCA.

26 Some of the Fingal resident landowners were PLGs of North Dublin union as they resided within its jurisdiction.

27 *Drogheda Independent*, 1891–8. Annual attendances as published in PLG minutes, *Drogheda Independent*, 1891–8. Unionists identified from attendance at Unionist Convention, Dublin, 1892.

28 Desmond McCabe Perrin, 'Perrin, Louis' in McGuire and Quinn (eds), *Dictionary of Irish biography*; Deane, *Weekly Irish Times*, 25 Feb. 1939; Hamlet, *Thom's Directory*, 1891, p. 1075.

29 *Drogheda Independent*, 22 July 1893.

30 Ibid., 26 Nov. 1892.

31 *Drogheda Independent*, 22 July 1893, discussion on amnesty for Fenian prisoners from Lismore PLU; 26 May 1894, similar resolution from Limerick corporation.

32 Ibid., 13 Aug. 1898.

33 Ibid., 14 Mar., 6 June 1891.

34 Ibid., 20, 27 June 1891, 27 Feb., 30 June 1892.

35 Ibid., 24 Sept., 8 Oct. 1892.

36 Marcus de Búrca, *The GAA: a history* (Dublin, 1980), pp 41–7; Richard McElligott, 'Richard Blake and the resurrection of the GAA, 1890–98', *Ríocht na Midhe: Records of the Meath Archaeological and Historical Society*, 24 (2013), 256–69.

37 *Census of Ireland, 1901. Part I. Area, houses, and population: the ages, civil or conjugal condition, occupations, birthplaces, religion, and education of the people. Vol. I. Province of Leinster*, HC 1902 [Cd. 847] cxxii, cxxiii.

38 W.F. Mandle, 'The GAA & popular culture, 1884–1924' in Oliver McDonagh, W.F. Mandle and Pauric Travers (eds), *Irish culture and nationalism, 1750–1950* (Basingstoke, 1983), p. 187; William Nolan (ed.), *The Gaelic Athletic Association in Dublin, 1884–1959* (Dublin, 2005), i, p. 25

39 *Dublin county board minute book, 1896–8*, p. 3, and 21 Oct., 15 Nov. 1893, pp 102–3, GAA/DUB/01/01, GAA archives, Croke Park; Nolan, *The GAA in Dublin*, pp 17–19.

40 Séamus Ó Maitiú, 'A spent force? An Claidheamh Soluis and the Gaelic League in Dublin 1893–1913' in Francis Devine (ed.), *A capital in conflict: Dublin city and the 1913 Lockout* (Dublin, 2013), pp 285–6.

41 Nolan, *The GAA in Dublin*, pp 72–7.

42 RIC inspector general and county inspectors' monthly confidential reports, *The British in Ireland*, CO 904, POS 8320: Feb. to July 1898.

43 Kettle, *Material for victory*, pp 120–2.

44 *Drogheda Independent*, 6 Apr. 1892.

45 *Land commission judicial rents, to March 1897*, HC 1897 [C. 8487] lxxxiv, 337, pp 96–9.

46 *Irish land commission (Purchase of Land (Ireland) Act, 1891). Return of advances under the act to the 31st March 1895*. HC (278) lxxxii, 161.

47 *Tuam Herald*, 21 Nov. 1890; *Irish Times*, 31 Jan. 1895.

48 *Kildare Observer*, 12 Mar. 1898.

49 *The Times*, 7 Mar. 1898.

2. ENERGY AND PURPOSE, 1899–1909

1 Michael Davitt, *The fall of feudalism* (London, 1904), p. 686.

2 Matthew Potter, *The municipal revolution in Ireland: a handbook of urban government in Ireland since 1800* (Dublin, 2010), pp 196–241; Desmond Roche, *Local government in Ireland* (3rd ed., Dublin, 1987).

3 John Joseph Clancy, *A handbook of local government in Ireland: containing an explanatory introduction to the Local Government (Ireland) Act, 1898* (Dublin, 1899).

4 Denis Gwynn, *The life of John Redmond* (London, 1932), p. 90. See also Pauric Travers, 'A bloodless revolution: the democratisation of Irish local government' in Mary Daly (ed.), *County and town: one hundred years of local government in Ireland* (Dublin, 2001), p. 12, which disputes this.

5 John Coakley, 'Local elections and national politics' in Daly (ed.), *County and town: one hundred years of local government in Ireland*, p. 77.

6 *Drogheda Independent*, 3, 17 Dec. 1898.
7 Maurice O'Keefe, *Irish life and lore: Fingal County collection*, CD 1 (2008); interview with Desmond O'Neill, Malahide, grandson of Joseph O'Neill, available at Fingal County Archives.
8 *Freeman's Journal*, 31 Dec. 1840.
9 Ibid., 21 July 1905; *Irish Times*, 2 Aug. 1913.
10 Thomas J. Morrissey, *Laurence O'Neill: lord mayor of Dublin, patriot and man of peace, 1864–1943* (Dublin, 2014).
11 Kettle, *Material for victory*, pp 14–17.
12 Desmond McCabe, 'Kettle, Andrew J.' in James McGuire and James Quinn (eds), *Dictionary of Irish biography* (Cambridge, 2009).
13 Kettle, *Material for victory*, p. xi.
14 Davitt, *The fall of feudalism*, p. 714.
15 *Drogheda Independent*, 14 Jan. 1899.
16 Ibid., 28 Jan., 1 Apr. 1899.
17 Travers, 'A bloodless revolution', pp 12–23.
18 Pauric Travers, *Settlements and divisions: Ireland, 1870–1922* (Dublin, 1988), p. 66.
19 Potter, *The municipal revolution*, p. 203.
20 *Slater's royal national directory of Ireland*, 1894, listing of Balbriggan town commissioners, p. 15
21 *Drogheda Independent*, 22 Apr. 1899.
22 Ibid., 8 Apr. 1899.
23 *Dublin county council minute books, 1899–1914*, FCCA/DCC/1.
24 *North Dublin R.D.C. minute books, 1899–1914*, FCCA/NDRDC 78/A.
25 *Dublin county council minute books, 1899–1914*, FCCA/DCC/1, 2 May 1899.
26 *Dublin county council minute books, 1899–1914*, FCCA/DCC/1, 13 June 1900, p. 75.
27 *Drogheda Independent*, 24 Jan. 1901.
28 Ciaran Wallace, 'Fighting for unionist home rule: competing identities in Dublin, 1880–1929', *Journal of Urban History*, 38 (2012), 936.
29 *Drogheda Independent*, 31 Mar. 1900.
30 Garry Ahern, *Portmarnock: its people and townlands* (Swords, 2013), p. 267.
31 *Drogheda Independent*, 17 Oct. 1903.
32 Myrtle Hill and John Lynch, 'Society and economy, 1870–1914' in Donnchadh Ó Corráin and Tomás O'Riordan (eds), *Ireland, 1870–1914: coercion and conciliation* (Dublin, 2010), pp 41–5.
33 *Return of advances made under the Irish land act, 1903*, July 1908, HC 1908 [Cd. 4490] p. 400; Aug. to Oct. 1909, HC 1908 [Cd. 5402] p. 477.
34 *Drogheda Independent*, 27 Oct. 1900, 16 Feb. 1901.
35 Curran Papers, MS 24, minute book of the North Dublin executive of the United Irish League (Thomas Kettle, secretary), 17 July 1902 to 17 Sept. 1903, p. 1.
36 *Drogheda Independent*, 1 Mar. 1902, 6 Dec. 1902, 7 Jan. 1905.
37 Ibid., 12 Dec. 1903; Desmond McCabe and Owen McGee, 'Daly, Patrick Thomas' and 'Egan, James Francis' in James McGuire and James Quinn (eds), *Dictionary of Irish biography* (Cambridge, 2009); Leon Ó Broin, *Revolutionary underground: the story of the Irish Republican Brotherhood, 1858–1924* (Dublin, 1976), pp 124–5.
38 *Drogheda Independent*, 17 Dec. 1904, 28 Jan. and 18 Feb. 1905.
39 Ibid., 21 May 1904.
40 *Dublin county board minute books, 1908–12*, GAA/DUB/01/02, 23 Mar. 1909, p. 20, 22; Feb. 1910, p. 72.
41 *Drogheda Independent*, 29 Mar. 1902.
42 Ibid., 26 Apr. 1902; Irish Unionist Alliance, *Unionist convention for Leinster Munster and Connaught proceedings* (Dublin, 1892).
43 *Drogheda Independent*, 13 and 27 May 1905, 9 June 1906.
44 Ibid., 31 Mar., 28 Apr. 1906.
45 Ibid., 27 July 1907, 30 May and 6 June 1908.
46 F.S.L. Lyons, 'The watershed,1903–7' in W.E. Vaughan (ed.), *A new history of Ireland*, vi: *Ireland under the union II, 1870–1921* (Oxford, 1996), pp 81, 111–22.
47 *Drogheda Independent*, 10 June 1905, 6 June 1908.
48 Ibid., Dec. 1905.
49 *Sinn Féin Weekly*, 26 Oct. 1907.
50 Richard P. Davis, *Arthur Griffith and non-violent Sinn Féin*, 'Sinn Féin executive members', pp 173–7; *Sinn Féin minute books, 1912–13*, UCDA P163, 23 Jan. 1913, UCD Archives.
51 *Sinn Féin Weekly*, 4 Apr., 9 May, 13 June 1908; *Irish Times*, 20 Sept. 1907.
52 Seán Ó Luing, *Art Ó Griofa* (Baile Átha Cliath, 1953), p. 179.

53 *Sinn Féin Weekly*, 2 May, 13 June 1908; *Drogheda Independent*, 29 Feb., 14 Mar. 1908; Ó Corráin and O'Riordan (eds), *Ireland, 1870–1914: coercion and conciliation*, p. 35.
54 *Drogheda Independent*, 21 Nov. 1908; Eugenio F. Biagini, *British democracy and Irish nationalism, 1876–1906* (Cambridge, 2007), p. 372.
55 For an account of early Sinn Féin, see Brian Feeney, *Sinn Féin: a hundred turbulent years* (Dublin, 2002) and Michael Laffan, *The resurrection of Ireland: the Sinn Féin party, 1916–1923* (Cambridge, 1999). Also Alvin Jackson, *Ireland, 1798–1998: politics and war* (Oxford, 1999), pp 142–274.
56 *Drogheda Independent*, 13 June, 11 July and 3 Oct. 1908.
57 *Irish Times*, 10 Mar. 1909, 31 May 1910

3. ON THE BRINK: NATIONAL AND LOCAL POLITICS CONVERGE, 1910–14

1 *Drogheda Independent*, 16 Apr. 1910.
2 Ibid., 26 Feb., 16 Apr. 1910, *Freeman's Journal*, 17 June 1914, 1901 Census, http://www.census.nationalarchives.ie/pages/1901/Dublin/Blackrock/Castledawson_Avenue/1313353.
3 'Ireland, civil registration indexes, 1845–1958', index, Family Search, https://familysearch.org/ark:/61903/1:1:FYHT-QPT (accessed 2 June 2015), marriage entry for Julia Lawless; citing Balrothery, Apr. to June 1894, vol. 2, p. 371, general registry, Dublin; FHL microfilm 101/257.
4 *Drogheda Independent*, 9 Apr., 11 June, 10 Dec. 1910.
5 *Irish Times*, 14 Feb. 1910, 29 June 1914; *Drogheda Independent*, 20 July, 24 Aug. 1912; RIC inspector general and county inspectors' monthly confidential reports, *The British in Ireland*, CO 904/87, POS 8338: May 1911.
6 *Drogheda Independent*, 3, 17 June 1911, 10, 15 June 1912.
7 Ibid., 4, 11, 25 Nov. 1911.
8 RIC inspector general and county inspectors' monthly confidential reports, *The British in Ireland*, CO 904/80–2, POS 8331–3: Jan. to Dec. 1910; CO 904/85–6, POS 8336–7: Jan. to Dec. 1911; CO 904/88, POS 8339: Dec. 1912; *Drogheda Independent*, 17 June 1911.
9 F.S.L. Lyons, 'The aftermath of Parnell, 1891–1903' in W.E. Vaughan (ed.), *A new history of Ireland*, vi: *Ireland under the union II, 1870–1921* (Oxford, 1996), p. 81.
10 *Freeman's Journal*, 20 May 1912.
11 Patrick Maume, *The long gestation: Irish nationalist life, 1891–1918* (Dublin 1999), pp 119–20.
12 Pauric Travers, *Settlements and divisions: Ireland, 1870–1922* (Dublin 1988), p. 78.
13 Michael Collins, Dáil Éireann Debates, vol. T, no. 6, 19 Dec. 1921.
14 *Drogheda Independent*, 16, 23 Aug., 7 Sept. 1912.
15 J.J. Lee, *The modernisation of Irish society, 1848–1918* (Dublin, 1973), pp 127–8.
16 Alvin Jackson, *Ireland, 1798–1998: politics and war* (Oxford, 1999), pp 152–3.
17 *Magistrates (Ireland). A return showing the names, addresses, occupations or descriptions of the persons appointed to the commission of the peace in Ireland since the 30th day of November, 1912, the date of the last return (parliamentary paper, no. 396, of session 1912–13), including all appointments to the end of 1913*, 1914 (461) lxvii, 1003; *Irish Times*, 22 May 1914.
18 E. McDowel Cosgrave and W.T. Pike, *Dublin and county Dublin in the twentieth century* (Brighton, 1908), p. 173; *Thom's Directory*, 1915, p. 1895.
19 Malahide Cricket Club website, http://www.malahidecc.com/pages/page_15377/history.aspx.
20 Donal Lowry, 'Kettle, Thomas Michael' in McGuire and Quinn (eds), *Dictionary of Irish biography*.
21 *Drogheda Independent*, 25 June 1913; *Irish Times*, 31 Jan. 1913.
22 RIC inspector general and county inspectors' monthly confidential reports, *The British in Ireland*, CO 904/89, POS 8340: Mar. 1913.
23 *Return of owners of land of one acre and upwards in counties, cities, and towns in Ireland*, HC 1876 [C. 1492] lxxx, 61. The biggest estates were Cobbe at Donabate, St Lawrence at Howth, Domville at Coolock, Woods at Balbriggan, Palmer at Rush, Holmpatrick at Abbotstown and Skerries, Hussey at Westown, Naul and Talbot at Malahide. While some

lands were sold between 1876 and 1913, these estates were still significant.

24 For a brief account of the farm labourers dispute, see E.A. Coyle, 'Larkinism and the 1913 County Dublin farm labourers dispute', *Dublin Historical Record*, 52:2 (2005), 176–90, and Gerard Hanley, 'Let the harvest go to blazes: farm labourers in North County Dublin and the 1913 Lockout' (MA, St Patrick's College, Drumcondra, 2014). For the city conflict, see Padraig Yeates, *Lockout: Dublin, 1913* (Dublin, 2001).

25 *Freeman's Journal*, 30 Sept. 1913.

26 *Irish Independent*, 1 Oct. 1913.

27 *Irish Times*, 29 Sept., 23 Oct. 1913.

28 Ibid., 29 Sept. 1913.

29 Ibid., 25 Feb. 1905.

30 *Drogheda Independent*, 27 Sept. 1913.

31 Christopher Lee, 'The principal rallying-ground for the Larkinites – the Swords riots of 1913', http://www.theirishstory.com/2013/07/15/the-principal-rallying-ground-for-the-larkinites-the-swords-riot-of-1913.

32 *Irish Independent*, 10 Oct. 1913.

33 *Freeman's Journal*, 17 Oct. 1913; *Drogheda Independent*, 18 Oct. 1913; *Weekly Irish Times*, 18 Oct. 1913; *Irish Independent*, 27 Oct. 1913.

34 General Prisons Board file on Frank Moss of the Irish Transport Union during his period in custody, Oct. 1913 to Feb. 1914, GPB/SFRG/1/24, National Archives of Ireland.

35 Maume, *The long gestation*, p. 129.

36 F.X. Martin and F.J. Byrne, *The scholar revolutionary: Eoin MacNeill, 1867–1945 and the making of the new Ireland* (Shannon, 1973), pp 146–7.

37 Diarmuid Lynch, *The IRB and the 1916 insurrection* (Cork, 1957), p. 24.

38 Ó Luing, *I die in a good cause*, pp 36–8.

39 *Drogheda Independent*, 21 Mar. 1914; Ann Matthews, *The Irish Citizen Army* (Cork, 2014), p. 36.

40 RIC inspector general and county inspectors' monthly confidential reports, *The British in Ireland*, CO 904/93, POS 8536: June 1914; Shane MacThomáis, *An Phoblacht*, 12 Dec. 2005.

41 *Irish Times*, 30 Apr. 1914.

42 *Irish Independent*, 10 June 1914; *Drogheda Independent*, 13 June, 11 July 1914.

43 RIC inspector general and county inspectors' monthly confidential reports, *The British in Ireland*, CO 904/94–5, POS 8537: July 1914.

44 *Drogheda Independent*, 18 Apr. 1914.

45 RIC inspector general and county inspectors' monthly confidential reports, *The British in Ireland*, CO 904/88, POS 8339: Oct. 1912; CO 904/90, POS 8341: May 1913.

46 Maume, *The long gestation*, p. 141.

47 Senia Pašeta, *Before the revolution* (Cork, 1999).

48 *Drogheda Independent*, 7 Sept. 1914.

49 *Freeman's Journal*, 9 July 1914; *Irish Independent*, 29 July 1914.

50 RIC inspector general and county inspectors' monthly confidential reports, *The British in Ireland*, CO 904/94, POS 8537: Aug. 1914.

51 BMH WS1399 Thomas Peppard. Rivalry was between the Rooney and the Taylor and Murtagh families.

52 Brendan Mac Giolla Choille, *Intelligence notes, 1913–1916* (Dublin, 1966), p. 112.

53 Military Service Pensions Collection: *Nominal Roll of 5th (Fingal) battalion, Dublin Brigade, Easter Week 1916*, MA/MSPC/RO/16.

54 www.census.nationalarchives.ie/pages/1901/Dublin/Blackrock/Castledawson_Avenue/1313353.

55 Committee of the Irish National War Memorial, *Ireland's memorial records, 1914–1918*, 8 vols (Dublin, 1923), http://search.ancestry.co.uk/cgi-bin/sse.dll?indiv=try&db=IrelandMemorial&h=5387.

56 *Irish Independent*, 26 Aug. 2005; BMH WS1438 Christopher Moran; http://irishmedals.org/fingal-volunteers.html.

57 Sean Ó Luing, *I die in a good cause: a study of Thomas Ashe – idealist and revolutionary* (Tralee, 1970), p. 27; http://www.blackravenpipeband.net/history.html.

58 http://trees.ancestry.co.uk/tree/12362004/person/-279034965/fact/6378443179; BMH WS 147 Bernard McAllister.

59 Nolan (ed.), *The GAA in Dublin*, pp 136, 153–60.

60 BMH WS1043 Joseph V. Lawless, pp 1–11; WS409 Valentine Jackson; WS386 Frank Gaskin; WS842 Sean Kennedy.

61 F.X. Martin, *The Irish volunteers, 1913–15: recollections and documents* (Dublin, 1963), p. 211; Pádraig Ó Snodaigh, *Comhghuaillithe na réabhlóide, 1913–1916* (Baile Átha Cliath, 1966), p. 124.

CONCLUSION

1 R.V. Comerford, *Ireland* (London, 2003), p. 1.
2 Leeann Lane, 'Ireland: identities and cultural traditions' in Mary McAuliffe, Katherine O'Donnell and Leeann Lane (eds), *Palgrave advances in Irish history* (Basingstoke, 2009), p. 240.
3 Emmet Larkin, 'Church, state and nation in modern Ireland', *American Historical Review*, 80 (1975) 1244–76, and 'The devotional revolution in Ireland, 1850–75', *American Historical Review*, 77 (1972), 625–52.
4 Larkin, *Church, state and nation in modern Ireland*, p. 1266.
5 John Hutchinson, *The dynamics of cultural nationalism: the Gaelic revival and the creation of the Irish nation state* (London, 1987).
6 Ibid., pp 169–70.
7 M.J. Kelly, *The Fenian ideal and Irish nationalism, 1882–1916* (Woodbridge, 2006).
8 See Sir Horace Plunkett, *Ireland in the new century* (London, 1904).
9 D. George Boyce, *Nineteenth-century Ireland: the search for stability* (Dublin, 1990), p. 216.
10 Hutchinson, *The dynamics of cultural nationalism*, p. 167.
11 For a brief biography of Kettle see Senia Paseta, *Thomas Kettle*, History Association of Ireland: Life and Times New Series (Dublin, 2008).
12 Comerford, *Ireland*, p. 266.
13 RIC inspector general and county inspectors' monthly confidential reports, *The British in Ireland*, CO/904, POS 8329: Jan. 1909.
14 Pauric Travers, *Settlements and divisions, Ireland, 1870–1922* (Dublin, 1988), p. viii.
15 *Irish Independent*, 19 Apr. 1922.
16 F.S.L. Lyons, 'The aftermath of Parnell' in Vaughan (ed.), *A new history of Ireland*, vi: *Ireland under the Union II, 1870–1921*, p. 81.